Image of the New Woman in the Novels of

Shobha De

CELEBRATING WOMEN'S WRITING

Image of the New Woman in the Novels of *Shobha De*

L. Sonia Ningthoujam

Prestige

an international publishing house

Published by
PRESTIGE BOOKS
3/28, East Patel Nagar
New Delhi 110 008
Ph. 9818755529

ISBN: 81-7551-171-0

Printed at Chaman Offset Press, New Delhi 110 002

CONTENTS

for

my loving parents

Mrs. and Mr. Mohendra Singh Ningthoujam

Preface

Of the many Indian-English writers Shobha De is one who occupies a distinctive place as a journalist and as a novelist in the literary scene in India. She is a popular novelist among the younger generation of readers in India and abroad. On account of her wide readership, she has been chosen as a writer deserving of detailed studies in academic institutions. It is not surprising that her novels have been selected to be read as course materials for graduate studies in Oriental and African Institute, London.

In most of her novels, De has been preoccupied with creating a new image of the woman who has been traditionally taken for granted as a weak, docile and submissive individual and for that reason suppressed and exploited by the male-dominated society. De endeavours to present the new woman as one who is daring, ambitious and aspiring, and is possessed of a great potential to realize her dreams and force upon the male-dominated world a due recognition of her identity. To achieve her goal, the new woman who represents the modern woman goes all out to exploit her potential, both physical and intellectual. It appears that De's new woman exploits her physical potential more daringly than women of other novelists. In this process she confronts her male counterpart in every field of activity where the latter had been enjoying unquestioned supremacy and domination through the centuries. The new woman strives to get total freedom from man if she finds any kind of hindrance or obstacles in achieving self-fulfillment. While carrying on this kind of struggle to achieve her goals, she recklessly overthrows traditionally established institutions such as marriage (husband-wife relationship), mother-child relationship, the sanctity of family, etc. In pursuing her goal of becoming rich and famous and creating legitimate and respectable space for herself in society she cannot but take, or is occasionally inclined to take, the feminist role of shattering established morality and creating a new kind of morality that appears sometimes staggering and unbelievable. She even uses her body as an important means to promote her ends caring little whether the traditional society would accept her ways.

The present book examines as analytically as possible the characteristic aspects of the aspirations and possibly the achievement of these aspirations of the new woman in all the seven novels that Shobha De has published so far. It is divided into six chapters, each chapter analyzing a different aspect in order to arrive at a composite picture of the image of the new woman in De's novels. In chapter one, I propose to deal with the writer and her works. This throws light on the development of her literary sensibility and her opinions as a writer. The next chapter deals with the writer vis-a-vis some other women novelists. It brings out the basic differences between the image of the traditional woman and that of the modern woman as De portrays her. It also takes note of the aspirations of the new woman and her strategies to achieve the same.

The third chapter deals with the aesthetic notions of De's women and the presentation of the new morality that is likely to emerge from her work. This chapter is devoted to emphasizing the aesthetic element in De's novels. It seeks to see how far the aesthetic perceptions and new morality of the new woman go hand in hand without creating any conflicting moral values in society.

In the fourth chapter the question of realism is dealt with at length to underline the kind of social and practical reality in which the new woman figures and creates a new image for herself in the present-day society. In what is perhaps a significant discussion of the novels in the last but one chapter of this book, I propose to evaluate the feminist stance in De's novels and analyze how she joins other literary feminist writers desiring to arouse the consciousness of the modern women in society, perhaps to show both the merits and shortcomings of the new image they are trying to create for themselves after the women's liberation movement.

The concluding chapter presents in sufficient detail a critical assessment of Shobha De's talent as a writer in order to examine what impression she has been able to create as a writer and how the reading public accepts her. It weighs the pros and cons of Shobha De's writing capability and opinions of literary critics about her writing.

I cannot close these prefatory remarks without thanking the people who made this project possible. At the very outset, I offer my heart-felt gratitude to Dr. S.K. Tikoo, Professor, Department of English, Manipur University, whose guidance and inspiration made this work come to a completion.

My sincere thanks are due to Dr. R.K. Dhawan of Delhi University who gave me valuable suggestions and study materials which helped me tremendously. My thanks are also due to the authorities of libraries of Delhi University, J.N. University, Delhi, and Manipur University.

I shall be failing in my duty if I do not express my deepest gratitude to my loving mother-in-law Smt. L. Sushila Devi, my parents Mr. and Mrs. N. Mohendra, my brothers Mahavir, Manikso, and brother-in-law Rahul. Last but not the least I must acknowledge my gratitude to my husband Mr. L.C. Somorendra, little son Siddhartha and all other family members without whose support and co-operation, this work would not have seen the light of the day.

Imphal **Sonia Ningthoujam**

Shobha De: Life and Works

Shobha De is a name to reckon with among the best known women novelists of India, for her upbeat non-conformist attitude in presenting the aristocratic urban Indian society in her novels. She is also one of India's best-selling authors. Born in an upper middle class family in Maharashtra in 1948, De completed her graduation in Psychology from St. Xavier's College, Mumbai. She became a model in the late Sixties much against the wishes of her bureaucrat father. In 1970 De took up a career in journalism and became the catty, fiery editor of the saucy film magazine *Stardust*. Using 'Hinglish', a peculiar anti-colonial mix of English and Mumbaite Hindi, the magazine won a wide following. "She also edited three popular magazines, namely, *Society* and *Celebrity*, and was consulting editor to *Sunday* and *Megacity*."[1] She earned herself name and fame with her brilliant writing skill as a free-lance writer, T.V. soap writer, and a columnist in leading newspapers and magazines. Physically charming at fifty-seven, she actively looks after her family of six kids and her husband and has the daily routine of writing for "six to eight hours."[2]

So far Shobha De has published twelve books out of which seven are novels. Her maiden novel *Socialite Evenings* (1989) is based on the lives of the super rich society of urban India. It became an instant hit and a bestseller. *Socialite Evenings* was written at the insistence of David Davidar, the editor and publisher of Penguin Books, India Division. This work was followed by a series of novels which have been trend setters in creating women characters defying traditional moral values. These novels are *Starry Nights* (1990), *Sisters* (1992),

Strange Obsession (1992), *Sultry Days* (1994), *Snapshots* and *Second Thoughts* (1996).

Shobha De is an extremely talented writer. In her novels she shows a great insight in giving a real picture of the Indian life-style and psyche. Her artistic maturity and purpose are evident in her writings. She dazzles the readers with her frank and candid tales of human relationships, particularly man-woman relationship and old and new value patterns. The changing moral values of people reaching new heights in riches and civilization is given an unrestrained depiction in her novels.

Yet, in her writing on sex Shobha is not restrained by social sanctions. To her sex is not something one need be ashamed of. In her fiction she is engaged in unravelling the dark and sinister sides of power, money and fame. Whatever she has presented, she has done it with a conviction that the readers may have a real feel of the life of people who are rich and powerful. The conservative section of the Indian society may no doubt condemn her writings as immoral. Yet she is not deterred by such criticism and is going strong with her writing. She is widely read by the new generation of Indian readers, especially the urban women who are fascinated with her writing. Because of her journalistic stints she is capable of writing more forcefully notwithstanding the brickbats she receives along with the laurels.

De seems to have won the hearts of people all over the world. In the *Toronto Review*, Paul W. Roberts observes:

> Staggeringly beautiful, she's also touchingly humble about her work. Looking into her eyes, I saw loneliness, passion, fear, humour, uncertainty, anger, sorrow and enormous strength. Not at once, but in succession, a reaction to circumstance—like a chameleon. Rarely have I encountered such windows into a soul opened so freely. What emerges is what one reads in her work: enigmatic, straightforward, crude, erudite, girlish, wise and ultimately contrived truth. She doesn't know how good a writer she is—which is why she is so good a writer.[3]

Again in *The Tribune*, De got another fitting praise for her works:

> She slaughters macho males with vengeance, and rattles poison in her gender with disdain and disregard. She is Shobha De, and she is scintillating and straight. She is a ruthless writer with a ramrod of a pen, and a raging urge to kill somebody. She demolishes reputations and civilizations with effortless grace, and one thing she doesn't stomach is hypocrisy of any kind. She wields a powerful camera, and she needs to keep shooting that way, whether anyone likes to photo frame or not.[4]

Born and brought up in a conservative middle class educated family she knows the pros and cons of belonging to that society. After graduating herself into the society of the rich and the famous, she acquired a better grasp of the experience of being a permanent member of that society, an experience she skilfully exploits in her novels. She has been using these wonderful bitter-sweet experiences—some of them her own and some gathered from the glittering social circle of Mumbai. Deeply involved with these social circles as she has been, she presents realistic and truthful images of this society in her novels.

Unlike other women novelists who have always shown a conscious restraint in writing about the physical side of man-woman relationship and also about the dark sides of loose morals in marital relationships, De evinces a daredevil courage in writing freely about sex, the new woman and society. Despite the harsh cries of protest from conservative critics, there is no doubt that there are hundreds of admirers of De who love her writings for their sheer candidness. The very fact that "her first three novels have been chosen by the reputed school of Oriental and African Studies in London as course material"[5] for graduate studies is enough proof that she has been able to create a stir in academic institutions not only in India but also abroad. In giving fictional images of both woman's and man's social reality, she lays bare a large chunk of the social reality which remained unexplored for a long time. As such it would be misleading to put any pornographic label on her writings. They are not to be regarded as explicit pages of pornography as some people allege.

De belongs to the modern feminist school of thought. She raises the women characters in her novels to be at par with male characters. They have an equal amount of independence in all walks of life. As De says: "I did write with a great deal of empathy toward women. Without waving the feminist flag, I feel very strongly about the woman's situation."[6]

De has drawn a real picture of the new woman who defies the age-old practice of suppression of women in almost all walks of life. Her women are strong enough to say a big 'no' to every unfair treatment meted out to them. They are a set of well-equipped women—filthy rich, well-educated, talented and unbelievably ambitious. De's women are powerful. They do not hesitate to challenge the socially approved male hegemony on the basic issues of life.

These women are calculative and use men as means to an end, the end being the fulfillment of their aim to become rich, famous and independent. The characters of almost all the women in her novels exhibit this quality. From Karuna and Anjali in *Socialite Evenings* to Maya in the most recent *Second Thoughts*, all have used man as their ladder to acquire riches and fame. These women show tremendous self-confidence in taking up all challenges to attain their desired goals. These women usher in a change in the customary attitude to moral values and demand a new definition of the woman's image. According to their perception a woman need not be unquestioningly docile and faithful to her husband or an epitome of sacrifice. Should the man be unfair in his treatment of her, she would be equally justified to reciprocate in yet more unfair terms. If the men have a wild sex life, the women in De's novels need be no less wild or less sexy. As shown by De such unfairly treated women can have a string of extra-marital affairs to counter the misconduct of their husbands. They may change their boyfriends as frequently as they change their designer dresses. In short, the social system based on male-domination is seriously threatened and called into question.

In her novels, De is all out to improve upon the traditional image of the Indian woman as a weak, docile person living at the mercy of her partner. She reshapes her women characters as aggressive blasters of the male ego and male hierarchy. As De observes: “The women in my books are definitely not doormats. They are not willing to be kicked around.”[7] De is of the firm belief that women will be men’s equal partner in all spheres of life. She visualizes that there will be a time when a woman’s voice will be universally heard and heeded. This is again evident from what she says: “The quarrel is not who will scramble to the top of the human heap and stay there but with the race being run in fair terms and without weighted handicaps. Men will have to come to terms with women power. This isn’t the voice of naive female optimism. It is the voice of reason and logic. I simply believe that another alternative just does not exist any longer.[8]

Shobha De has created a rapport with the new generation of readers with her frank and realistic writings on urban high society life. She aims at figuring out the new woman who will be a force to reckon with in this society. No doubt, the projected image of this new woman has both the positive and negative sides to her personality in her novels. Interpreted in a positive light De’s novels may be seen as her various artistic endeavours to give the message that these women though admirable and commendable yet need to keep a balance in their overly independent life-style and make life more purposeful. Their talents may not be spent merely in tracking down the rich and powerful men or in spurning their gorgeous diamonds and rubies. Her novels are intriguing, and blatantly truthful images of the upcoming new woman with an amazing potential for progress or fall in her relationship with men and society. This new woman is an aberration from the usual representation of women characters by other women novelists of India.

Indian woman over the ages has been an image of tolerance, sacrifice and purity. She has always occupied a place secondary to man who lords over her as her master. Ours is a male-dominated society. Men rule over women despite the fact that there have been so many reforms and changes in the modern world through education and learning. Her identity as an individual is not yet fully accepted. Her demand for rights and equality has gained acceptance in Western countries to a very large extent. Women in these places are much more emancipated than their counterparts in Asia. In India too the female voice for power and equality is gradually rising higher. The importance of participation of women in the growth and development of the human society is shown by Sarojini Naidu. As Naidu observed: "Other national questions come and go; they are result of the time changing spirit: but one question that has never changed since the beginning of time itself, and life itself, is the duty of womanhood, the influence of womanhood, the sanctity of womanhood, the simple womanhood as the divinity of God upon earth, the responsibility of womanhood in shaping the divinity into daily life."[9]

The importance of giving woman a dignified place in society has also been voiced by great men of India like Gandhiji, Tagore and Swami Vivekananda. Tagore had said: "Women should acquire pure knowledge for becoming a more mature human being and utilitarian knowledge for becoming a true woman."[10] And this is possible only when "All sleeping women will awake now and move,"[11] as they used to be in ancient times.

The importance of focussing on women's issues is clearly seen in the works of Indian women novelists who have created different types of images of the Indian woman over the years. The image of Indian woman in the novels of these women novelists is varied, colourful, intense and wonderfully interesting. This may be because of the fact that these women writers focus mainly on women's issues in their writings and view the world from a woman's perspective. They have painted the different issues of the Indian woman from traditional and modern viewpoints depicting all her desires, anxieties, happiness and sorrow, defeat and victory and focussed the woman's inner world and her position in society.

Women writers like Amrita Pritam, Kamala Das, Kamala Markandaya, Anita Desai, Nayantara Sahgal, Shobha De and, more recently, Arundhati Roy have written on the Indian woman and her successes and failures in the society. An Indian critic has rightly said: "In India also, women authors have boldly come out with intimate details of their lives in their autobiographies. When women could talk so freely about themselves, it was natural that they would be more uninhibited in their writings, especially in their novels."[12]

Amrita Pritam is one such well-known writer and champion of the cause of women who has given frank and unrestrained account of her intimate relationships with different men at different times in her autobiography, *Raseedi Ticket*[13] (*Revenue Stamp*). In a very intimate manner, she describes her infatuation for the Urdu poet Sahir Ludhianwi and a similar passion which Sajjad Zahir had for her. Another well-known woman writer is Kamala Das who narrates in her autobiography, *My Story*, about her engagement and how her fiancé had behaved with her: "pushed me into a dark corner behind a door and kissed me sloppily near my mouth. He crushed my breasts with his thick fingers. Don't you love me, he asked me, . . . I felt hurt and humiliated."[14]

These examples show the courage with which the Indian women authors reveal what a woman has to face in a male-dominated society. Yet discussing these autobiographies is not enough. To get a real picture of Indian womanhood it is always better to go for a broader view in the novels where it is seen most clearly.

In Kamala Markandaya's novels, the Indian woman defines herself by a set of relationships and modes of conduct within a created society. "Despite the changes in norms, the impact of western culture, and alien mores, economic and social progress, she is essentially Indian in sensibility."[15] Kamala Markandaya brings out the traditional attitude of women in her novels. Her women characters are these suppressed and thwarted women who still dare to question the status quo and strive to assert their individuality. Her novels, *Nectar in a Sieve* and *A Silence of Desire* show the plight of Indian woman in the face of traditional patriarchal norms.

Anita Desai is another woman novelist who has brought out the Indian woman's inner world in her novels. Her novels *Voices in the City*, *Where Shall We Go This Summer?* and *Cry, the Peacock* show the author's urge for a way of living which would respond to the innermost yearnings of the Indian woman for self-emancipation and self-dignity. Desai states in an article on women writers: "the literary achievements of Indian women are severely limited because of their poverty of experience and improper physical and mental exercise"[16]

Another prominent Indian woman writer is Nayantara Sahgal. She is best known for her novels *This Time of Morning*, *Storm in Chandigarh* and *The Day in Shadow*. In her novels the women characters protest against the society's denial of freedom to them and the outdated social opinion and orthodox treatment. The heroines in the above novels are wives of social high-ups, very sensitive and anxious for individual freedom. Sahgal's female characters are deeply rooted in Indian culture and they struggle to be free and full human beings in their own rights. Sahgal makes Simrit in *The Day in Shadow* come out vehemently: "I hate this country except for the freedom it brought for countries and people, especially for women. But it is barbaric otherwise, full of rotten, elastic standards and the worship of money. I hate the whole mass of human affairs."[17]

One of the latest women writers to join this brigade is Arundhati Roy. Her novel *The God of Small Things* won her the coveted Booker Prize making her the first Indian woman to receive this prize. It gives a vivid detail of the changing political scene in Kerala, the problems faced by women in a male-dominated society, caste taboos, the lives of neglected and directionless children of a broken home, sex and also immensely captivating descriptions of birds, flowers and trees. "In *The God of Small Things*, Roy implicitly presses for greater social reform in the rigid positioning of women and the intolerable plight of the deprived class. She narrates the pain and misery of a lonesome mother in an indifferent world perceived through the eyes of her seven-year-old child—a world where the age-old subjugation of women and the indescribable humiliation of the under class still persist."[18]

Women writers have been enthusiastically engaged in bringing about a radical social change and demanding recognition of the woman's position and potentiality in the development of the human society.

This study proposes to throw light on the image of the new woman in the novels of Shobha De. Even though there have been a number of presentations of women in the works of other Indian women novelists, De's image of the new woman stands apart from the rest. The new woman in her novels stands for the modern woman who aspires for achieving equality with man in all spheres of life. Her revolt against the traditional notions of morality and aesthetics is pervasive in her novels. She aspires for these goals and her rights at any cost and so creates a new image of herself in the modern society and the world. She looks for fame, riches, contacts and power.

The present study is divided into six chapters, each chapter analyzing a different aspect in order to arrive at a composite picture of the image of the new woman in De's novels. In chapter one I propose to deal with the background to the writer's work as a novelist. This will throw light on the development of her literary sensibility and her opinions as a writer. The next chapter intends to deal with the writer vis-a-vis some other women novelists. This chapter is intended to bring out the basic differences between the traditional image of woman and the modern woman as De portrays it. It also takes note of the aspirations of the new woman and her strategies to achieve the same.

The next chapter will deal with the aesthetic notions of De and the presentation of the new morality that is likely to emerge from her work. This chapter is devoted to emphasizing the aesthetic element in De's novels. It seeks to see how far De's aesthetics and new morality go hand in hand without creating any conflicting moral values in society.

In the next chapter, the question of realism is dealt with at length to underline the kind of social and practical reality in which the new woman figures and creates a new image for herself in the present-day society. In what is going to be an important discussion of the novels in the last but one chapter of this book, I propose to evaluate the feminist stance in De's novels and analyze how she joins other literary feminist writers desiring to arouse the consciousness of the modern women, perhaps to show them both the merits and the shortcomings of the new image they are trying to create for themselves after the women's liberation movement.

The concluding chapter will present a critical assessment of Shobha De's talent as a writer in order to examine what impression she has been able to create as a writer and how the reading public accepts her. It weighs the pros and cons of Shobha De's writing capability and opinions of some of the distinguished literary critics.

In the light of this background I intend to analyze the various facets of her novels which intrigue the younger generation of readers everywhere. It would be pertinent to have a precise view of the manner in which Shobha De contrasts the traditional and modern women which I shall undertake to examine in my next chapter.

NOTES

1. R.S. Pathak, "Feminist Concerns in Shobha De's work: A Study in Attitudes," *The Fiction of Shobha De*, ed. Jaydipsinh Dodiya (New Delhi: Prestige, 2000), p. 35.
2. Surabhi Khosla, "The New Age of Women Authors," *The South-Asian.com*, Feb. 2002.
3. Paul W. Roberts, *Toronto Review*, qtd. *Shooting from the Hip* (New Delhi, 1996).
4. *The Tribune*, on *Shooting from the Hip* (New Delhi, 1996), n.p.
5. Jaydipsinh Dodiya and R.K. Dhawan, "The Fiction of Shobha De: An Introduction," *The Fiction of Shobha De*, ed. Jaydipsinh Dodiya, p. 15.
6. *Ibid.*, p. 14.
7. Ajay Singh, "The Trouble with Men," *Asia Week*, n.d.
8. Shobha De, *Shooting from the Hip*, p. 113.
9. B.G. Kher, *The Pageant of Life* (Ahmedabad, 1959), p. 58.
10. Rabindranath Tagore, "Man and Woman: Wings of Death," *Light from the East: An Anthology of Asian Literature: Japan, Korea, Vietnam and India*, ed. W.M. Naughton (New York, 1978), p. 94.
11. Yosawro Akiko, "The Day," *Ibid.*, p. 28.
12. Sharad Srivastava, *The New Woman in Indian English Fiction: A Study of Kamala Markandaya, Anita Desai, Namita Gokhale and Shobha De* (New Delhi, 1996), p. 1.
13. Amrita Pritam, *Raseedi Ticket* (New Delhi, 1993), p. 85.
14. Kamala Das, *My Story* (New Delhi, 1977), p. 85.
15. P. Geetha, "The Novels of Kamala Markandaya: Reassuring Feminine Identity," *Between Space of Silence: Women Creative Writers*, ed. Kamini Dinesh (New Delhi, 1994), p. 126.
16. Anita Desai, "Women Writers," *Quest*, 65 (April/June 1970), p. 40.
17. Nayantara Sahgal, *The Day in Shadow* (New Delhi, 1976), p. 35.
18. Bimaljit Saini, "*The God of Small Things*: A Feminist Analysis," *Indian Writing in English*, ed. Manmohon K. Bhatnagar, Vol. 5 (New Delhi, 1991), p. 171.

Traditional Woman versus Modern Woman: A Study of Shobha De's Novels

Tradition has a very strong hold over the Indian society and even a stronger hold over its women folk. Moreover the society is basically a Hindu society where women are given a status lower than that of men. Traditional rules and norms bind the Indian women in nearly every quarter.

Indian tradition over the centuries has regarded woman as preserver of the family. She makes all kinds of sacrifices for the welfare of the family. Right from her childhood she is taught that her main duty is to obey. A number of social evils infested the Indian society in the eighteenth, nineteenth and the early part of the twentieth century. The evil practice of Sati was prevalent. When the husband died, the wife followed him by joining him on the funeral pyre. Even if the wife was very young, her wish to live was strangled and went unheeded. By compulsion she had to die with her husband, to become a Sati. This cruel custom was part of Pativrata Dharma so as to prove her faithfulness towards her husband. The narrow outlook of the people also prompted this practice. It was thought that if the widow happens to be young she might be a slur on the family by her undesirable conduct. Moreover, people generally thought that, as long as she lived she would be a burden on the family. Even very recently, in the later part of the twentieth century, a Sati case in Rajasthan shook the entire country. The burning of Roop Kunwar, a young bride, on the funeral pyre of her husband only shows how orthodox our society is even when science has proved a number of such age-old beliefs to be useless and harmful to the society.

To be born a girl in this society was like a curse. The birth of a son was welcome and celebrated with great enthusiasm and the birth of a daughter was shunned and considered as foreshadowing a chain of troubles for the parents. As such girls were married off early before they reached the age of puberty. Parents of the girl child worried about who their daughter would marry but were not bothered about educating her. It was only after she was packed off in marriage that they felt relieved of the burden of having her in the family. Many infants were killed as soon as they were born if they were found to be girls.

The dowry system, which emerged from the sacred ritual of marrying off the daughter and sending her along with some gifts to her husband's house, took an ugly form with the passage of time. Families came to be ruined due to high dowry demands made by the bridegrooms. Marriage became almost like an auction in the open market. Wives were burnt by their husbands and in-laws if they could not fetch the dowry they demanded. Unable to withstand the inhuman treatment meted out to them a number of these women committed suicide. Even though dowry demanding is a crime punishable by law, this practice goes on even in the present time. The high and mighty class of our society is the worst follower of this evil custom. A woman without dowry in marriage is regarded as incomplete.

However, this traditional perception about women has undergone an important change. The narrow outlook towards women has greatly changed with the passage of time. The first reformists who came out for the cause of women were Ishwar Chandra Vidyasagar, Swami Dayanand, Swami Vivekananda, Raja Rammohun Roy, Sir Syed Ahmed Khan, Keshav Chandra Sen and others. They brought about women's emancipation in our conservative society by trying to wipe out Sati,

Purdah, child marriage, dowry system and other evil practices. Education became not only men's field but women's too. Education played an important role in bringing Indian women into the mainstream of development. As Swami Vivekananda said: "All nations have attained greatness by paying proper respect to women. That country and that nation which did not respect women has never become great, nor will ever in future. The principal reason why your race is so much degraded is that you had no respect for these living images of Shakti."[1]

After men first came forward for the cause of women, women were encouraged to bring about reforms. Well known among them are Pandita Ramabai Saraswati, Anandibai Joshi and Mrs. Annie Besant. These reformation movements for women emancipation directly helped in producing a class of women who were totally different in their attitude and outlook from the traditional women of conservative India.

Literature underwent a significant change with the emergence of these visionary women in society. Literature which was till recently dominated by the males started reflecting the sparks that emanated from their struggle to realize their identity. Women who were previously imprisoned in the walls of the family shackled by tradition now looked upon themselves from a different angle.

Rabindranath Tagore elaborates on the problems of the women of his age in his novels. His writings are focussed on the plight of widows, struggle of modern educated women for equality and freedom in the male-dominated society and also on the complications that developed when the modern women participated in the freedom struggle. His novel *Two Sisters* shows his classification of wives. The first category comprises wives of the mother type and the other that of the beloved type.

Asha, Kamala and Sharmila are traditional women. Kamala is a typical Indian housewife who is completely immersed in the Hindu tradition and is comparable to Sita and

Savitri. She belongs to that class of women who evidence unquestioned faith in their husbands. They regard it a sin even to think about another man. Asha though a woman of the traditional type like Kamala has an individuality of her own. She loves her husband with sincerity and serves him loyally with devotion. But the moment he proves to be unfaithful to her, she throws away his divine image and despite her mother-in-law's prompting to win back her husband. Asha is different from Sharmila who is prepared to allow her husband to remarry the woman of his choice, who shockingly happens to be her own sister. Such women have motherly affection and love for their husbands. They believe that "Husband can do no wrong. For them their husbands are their gods."[2]

Raja Rao, another prominent Indian-English writer, regards maternity as the most sacred of earthly manifestations. Rama in *The Serpent and the Rope* regards Madeleine's pregnancy with awe. He says: "She was not mine, maternity had given her an otherness, she seemed secretive and incommunicable."[3]

Little mother is so much synonymous with motherhood that she is not given a separate name. Her study of the shastras, the Vedic scriptures, had prepared her for her role in life. Raja Rao also wants to show that modern woman, both eastern and western—that is, Saroja and Madeleine—are troubled as they cannot identify themselves with the traditional values without questioning them. The implicit faith in tradition that the little mother has cannot be expected in a person exposed to cross-cultural patterns. Savitri and Saroja try to abide by the ideals of Hindu cultural milieu but they find themselves as misfits.

An extraordinary variety of feminine temperament is encountered in the works of another veteran Indian-English writer R.K. Narayan. The joint family is a peculiar feature of Indian society and Narayan makes ample use of it. Sumati and Kamala in *The Dark Room* differ from one another; the older is weak, the younger spirited. But both suffer when their parents quarrel. The mother's misery is reflected on the daughters: they become miserable and are faced with so many restrictions, especially the inability to go out freely. Again, in *Waiting for Mahatma*, Bharti is bold, but the feeling of love comes out quite late in her heart. In Ashram she does not commit herself to Bapu's consent. Thus, it is not common for girls from middle class families to express love or make their decisions. Rosie in R.K. Narayan's *The Guide* is a modern woman who defies tradition to get what her heart yearns for—to become a dancer leaving her husband and taking help from another man who later develops an illicit relationship with her. Raju gets a niche in her heart precisely because of his appreciation of her art. Later, feeling guilty of breaking up her marital bond, she sits up at night repentant of her conduct towards her husband: "After all, after all, he is my husband. . . . Any other husband would have throttled me then and there."[4]

Some Indian male writers have also taken interest in dealing with the women issues to bring about their better understanding and awareness in our male-dominated society. They have done a commendable service to women by their writings.

Women's issues have been picked by women writers with a lot more enthusiasm than expected in a bid to support the cause of women's liberation. Through these women writers' eyes we can see a totally new world. Traditional ways and values and modern life-styles find a prominent place in the portrayal of women characters by these women novelists. "Women who conform to the existing moral ethics and code and social norms, especially with regard to their relationship with men and reactions to familial frictions, are certainly traditionalist. Those who defy traditions and opt for modernity are non-conformists. Conformity to a pattern does not mean dumb acceptance of all that is thrust on them. It takes for granted a certain degree of willingness and whole-hearted acceptance. Conformists hold on to the set of traditional values; sometimes, even at the cost of individual happiness. A tradition-abiding woman even sacrifices her happiness for the well being of the family, but at the same time retains her individuality."[5]

"Women of the oriental tradition are in general adjustable, accommodative, pliable and service-minded."[6] Among them the Indian woman is more tradition bound. She is ever ready to serve her family unquestioningly. To her the well-being and happiness of the family rise above everything else and she does not even think once when she sacrifices all her desires and happiness for the sake of all those who call her the custodian of their family's honour and prestige.

The modern woman does not find any sense in being acquiescent. She is not ready to suffer and sacrifice as the traditional Indian woman does. She wants to project her image as an individual, free from all kinds of conservative thinking which she seeks to overthrow. She is ready to fight her way against all odds coming in her way in fulfilling her aspirations. She rebels against the existing moral codes and social norms which either in theory or in practice tend to relegate the woman to a secondary place in society. Her rebellious craving for individuality and happiness cannot but result in the break up of family and relationships within the family.

In the novels of the women writers we come across a varied hue of Indian women—traditional, both traditional and modern, and the ultra-modern non-conformists. Traditional women who still retain their individuality are seen in the novels of Kamala Markandaya. Women who face challenges in their quest for self-fulfillment are portrayed in the novels of Nayantara Sahgal. Women who opt for modernity for convenience and not out of conviction are seen in the characters of Ruth Prawer Jhabvala. Women who use modernity as a licence for licentiousness can also be seen in her novels. Women who are traditional, oppressed, exploited and tortured in the name of tradition are found in the women characters of Arundhati Roy. Shobha De's women are ones who form a new and highly intriguing group—they are daring, educated, unconventional, shrewd, rich, and self-absorbing with loose morals.

Kamala Markandaya's women characters are both conformists and traditionalist. Women are the central figures in most of her novels. In four of her novels: *Nectar in a Sieve*, *Some Inner Fury*, *Possession* and *Two Virgins*, the central consciousness is that of a woman. Her novels are characterized by a fine feminine sensibility. Markandaya's women are well drilled in the tenets of Indian ethos. They possess an admirable strength to face the calamities of life and are adept at the wisdom of compromise and adjustment.

Rukmani in *Nectar in a Sieve* impresses us with her amazing capacity to compromise with the harsh facts of life. They emerge neither as a result of her actions nor because of her failures. There is no passivity in Rukmani's acceptance but only a strong conviction. It is not stoic resignation but heroic acceptance. She believes: "We would be pitiable creatures indeed to be so weak, for, is not man's spirit given to him to rise above his misfortunes."[7] Again, Rukmani is passionately attached to her husband and fondly loves her children. She even forgives his affairs with Kunthi and serves him till his death. She is both traditional and a conformist.

Sarojini in *A Silence of Desire* too gets her strength and sustenance from her religious beliefs. Sarojini is calm and quiet, serene and submissive. Her husband Dandekar is made aware of the presence of the virtues in his placid wife—her strong will, assertive nature and obduracy. The idleness of Dandekar brings out the chasm between the two. Dandekar realizes that there is no real understanding between them and that makes his wife withdraw from him and suffer. She had visited the Swami secretly because, as she feared: "You would have called me superstitious, a fool because I have beliefs you cannot share. You would not have let me be, no, you would have reasoned until I lost my faith because faith and reason do not go together and without faith I shall not be healed."[8] Dandekar does not comprehend the strength of her conviction. For all her devotion to the Swami, Sarojini is still a dutiful wife and a responsible mother. "She worked strenuously and slept as little as she could to make up for the time she spent away."[9] She faces Dandekar's accusation of infidelity with complete calmness. This is the result of her innate strength which emanates from her conviction that what she has been doing is right. Sarojini's acceptance of tradition does not make her a weakling. She retains her individuality.

Nalini in *A Handful of Rice* suffers passively the savage treatment by her husband Ravi; her husband unable to face the economic problems gives vent to his frustration on his docile and submissive wife. And Nalini accepts adversity passively: "Nalini took it stoically. She was used to obedience and saw no point in hanging her head against a stone wall."[10]

Nalini points out to Ravi that he is being influenced by Damodar who is a bad man. Ravi hardly listens. She leaves home out of frustration but comes back the moment Ravi calls her back. Even if her compromise appears to be the result of her helpless situation, there seems to be enough wisdom in her acceptance. For she knows that rebellion and defiance would not have shown her a way out of suffering and poverty.

Vasantha in *The Nowhere Man* is Indian to the core. She is proud of her Indian roots and refuses to leave it and embrace the new English culture. To her, material well-being is nothing in comparison with human values. She sticks to her Indian ways of living and dressing. She clings to her identity and refuses to give up her individuality. While Srinivas wants to identify himself with the country he adopts as his own, she chooses to cling to her identity till the end. She wants to be an Indian even in death. She is a loving and dutiful wife yet fiercely individualistic in her belief and behaviour.

These women who conform to the existing traditions seem to have been modelled on the mythical characters of Sita and Savitri—symbols of sacrifice, suffering and true love for the spouse. Like their role models, they retain their individuality despite being tradition-bound.

Women writers in English present with great insight and understanding the dilemma which is faced by women in a traditional society where dual morality is the accepted norm. Self-willed and individualistic women face suffering caused by broken relationships. Women who are aware of their emotional needs and strive for self-fulfilment rejecting existing traditions and social set up are seen in the novels of Nayantara Sahgal. These women long for liberty and want a new social order where they can be what they want to be, where there is no need for hypocrisy, and where character is judged by the purity of the heart and not by the chastity of the body. Almost all her novels portray women who embrace this new concept of modernity.

In Nayantara Sahgal's *Storm in Chandigarh*, Saroj looks at her pre-marital affairs as a part of growing up, as a part of learning. But her husband Inder cannot accept it easily. He continues to harbour the thought of Saroj's impurity even after four years of their marriage and having two children. All her attempts to get back Inder's love and companionship fail. Inder has an affair with Mara and Saroj with Vishal. Inder has a physical relationship with Mara but objects to his wife's friendship with Vishal. Saroj fights back by developing a relationship with Vishal. Nayantara Sahgal's women are strivers and aspirers toward a kind and compassionate world. Even though Saroj opts for a break with Inder, she is very traditional in that she is gentle, patient, homely and affectionate. She walks out of marriage only when it proves more of a bondage than a partnership.

In *A Day in Shadow*, Simrit's desire to be her own self culminates in separation from Som, her husband. It is the clash of ideals more than the clash of personalities. Even after getting herself freed of the marital bond, Simrit suffers. It is in fact the beginning of a battle with the agreed terms of divorce weighing her down. If Vishal Dubey's friendship provides the necessary strength to Saroj to protest against injustice, it is Raj who uncarves Simrit and makes her aware that she can make political choices. Simrit walks out of her marriage hoping for a brighter, friendlier world where she will be accepted with her ideals. Nayantara writes, "I try to create the virtuous woman, the modern Sita, if you like. My women are strivers and aspirers toward freedom, toward goodness, toward a compassionate world. Their virtue is a quality of heart and mind and spirit, a kind of untouched innocence and integrity. I think there is this quality in the Indian women." Sex for her women characters is not an appetite, it is a fulfillment.[11]

Ruth Prawer Jhabvala's women constitute yet another group which proclaims to be modern and refuses to conform. They have a fascination for modernity. It is surprising that after walking on to the new path of modernity for sometime, they again come back to their traditional path.

In *Esmond in India*, Shakuntala in her craze for the new English fashions takes to poetry and art and even feels for Esmond who is already married to another woman Gulab. For Shakuntala, marriage with Esmond is very desirable for she is fascinated with the idea that she will be marrying a divorcee who happens to be a foreigner. Besides, according to her perception, to be a divorcee is glamorous and a sign of advancement.

Again, Gulab's character is also very inconsistent. She had married Esmond much against her family's objections. After the initial attraction wears off, her husband begins to ill-treat her. Later she shrinks from society with almost pathological fear.

In *Get Ready for Battle*, Kusum a beautiful widow seeks to entrap another woman's husband. She does everything in her power to bring in a divorce between Gulzarilal and Sarla Devi, so that she could marry Gulzarilal. She throws away social acceptability to the winds and starts living with the man. Kusum is shown defying all traditions and doing everything in the name of modernity to fulfil her lustful desire for Gulzarilal.

Again, Arundhati Roy in her novel *The God of Small Things* portrays women in a traditional male-dominated society. Her women characters are seen to be suffering the age-old subjugation and humiliation of the underclass. In *The God of Small Things*, Roy implicitly presses for greater social reform in the rigid positioning of women and the intolerable plight of the deprived class. The character of Mamachi is that of a submissive and meek traditional wife who falls prostrate at the feet of her husband. She is beaten by her husband every night: "Every night he beats her with a brass flower vase. The beatings weren't now. What was new was only the frequency with which they took place."[12] She does not complain but takes it as a normal part of her marriage and their marriage survives long enough till Papachi dies. Her daughter Ammu is restless to break free from the restrictive behaviour at home, mainly Papachi's outbursts of physical violence to Mamachi from time to time. She gets no real freedom but just a change of master. Her husband too dominates her like her father does to her mother. She decides to walk out of her marriage unable to withstand her husband's violence after getting drunk.

Ammu has no alternative but to return home where she stays like an unwelcome guest. Ammu finds love and solitude in Velutha's arms much against the family's objection. Velutha's low social standing comes much in her way. They are condemned and Ammu dies in isolation while Velutha bleeds to his death due to police torture. The traditional helpless woman is shown suffering till she dies while the class-ridden orthodox society revels in its patriarchal power.

In this study, modern woman is a woman who defies tradition and society and comes to have a new identity. Women of her type are heroines in Shobha De's novels. These women comprise a small but prominent cross-section of society. They belong to the world of the rich and the powerful. They are usually wives and daughters of rich business tycoons and rich bureaucrats, women of the corporate world, famous film actresses and others. They are a new breed of women who live life on their own terms. For instance, an image of the new woman is thus presented by Shobha De: "The scene was changing, even in Bombay. Women worked, women married, women divorced and women remained single."[13]

These modern women love to be treated like queens wherever they go. They command attention and indulgence from men and people they come in contact with. Men follow them like dogs. These women drive the trendiest cars; they go to expensive hotels to wine and dine; they even prefer shopping outside their own country and travel abroad. They go to the finest tourist resorts to spend the summer. These women do not have any fixed time for returning home like their traditional counterparts who do not move out of their houses except for marketing or going to temple or to their office if they happen to be working women. The morals of these modern women are questionable. They appear to have thrown chastity out of their windows and share beds with a chain of lovers. De portrays these women in her novels with great enthusiasm and accuracy. She has herself been a person who has walked shoulder to shoulder with these people and has risen to fame and glory portraying these very people. Shobha De knows every individual of this bright glittering world.

Socialite Evenings which is Shobha De's first novel shows the kind of life led by these modern women. The women characters in this novel live a life of fun, enjoyment and self-indulgence regardless of the pain and unhappiness that are bound to come by having led such reckless lives. All they care about is their status and wealth.

In *Socialite Evenings*, the women characters are non-conformists. Anjali and Karuna are women who have left their conventional Indian middle class homes in search of freedom—a freedom which is not bound by any rule, a freedom unlimited and overflowing. They are ambitious and daring. They marry for convenience and are little bothered about what type of person their man will turn out to be in the long run or how long their marriage will last. They feel no scruples in fixing up extra marital connections even when their marriages are intact.

Anjali marries Abe (Abas Tyabji) for he is rich and so could give her all the luxury that she had dreamt of. Anjali knew beforehand that Abe had a wild reputation with women. Anjali is unhindered; to her Abe is the golden egg-laying goose. She even procures young virgins for Abe's sexual satisfaction. Anjali is not at all jealous when Abe takes a new girl to bed. These are like routine work and Anjali is used to it. In a beach party Abe openly shows off his dirty carnal habit:

> The bhang was working its dangerous magic on everyone. Abe and the woman start to lurch drunkenly across a narrow retaining wall along the edge of the property. He was yelling, 'Why don't you remove your top and I take off my bottom and we become one?' (31)

Anjali has her own set of lovers. Like her husband she is equally reckless in her sexual behaviour. She develops illicit relationship even with a very young boy who, age-wise, could well be her son but the affair ends in a disaster. She picks up another affair, this time with a Frenchman. After it too ends disastrously she marries Kumar, a gay who has plenty of money. Life to Anjali means only men and money.

Karuna too leads a wild, reckless life ever since she comes out of her strictly traditional, middle class home. Much against the wishes of her father, she joins the shunned world of modelling. With Anjali as her mentor she plunges into the wild glossy world of an upper social circle in Mumbai. Like Anjali, Karuna too marries for money. But her dreams are tarnished because her husband turns out to be a typical Indian male who has little consideration for the wishes of his wife. In desperation Karuna picks up her husband's friend Krish to satisfy her sexual urges. She openly goes with Krish for a holiday in Venice. This is an unthinkable step to any self-respecting Indian woman of a conservative background. She gets divorce from her husband and takes up a career in advertising. She succeeds in carving out a niche for herself in this competitive world. She becomes financially independent and this becomes her extra asset to flirt unlimited. She involves herself with Ranbir Roy, a much-married journalist.

To these women marriage and family do not count. All is for convenience and fun. All they crave for is unlimited liberty. This is the image of the new woman that De creates in her novels.

In De's *Starry Nights*, Aasha Rani is inducted into the glittering Bombay film world by her own mother. Aasha Rani's mother (Amma) is a strange character who in her hunger for fame and wealth goes all out to sell her daughter's chastity. She takes Aasha Rani from one film producer to another wearing indecent dresses to draw on their weakness and have them sign her daughter in their films looking only at her physical assets rather than her acting talent. Aasha Rani undoubtedly succeeds and flourishes in the film industry using her body as a bait for catching big producers and directors' attention. As she confesses to film financier Kishenbhai: "You financed and produced my first film Kishenbhai, but you extracted payment from my body."[14]

No girl from a decent conservative traditional family will think of joining the tinsel world at the cost of her chastity. Aasha Rani rises to the position of a top heroine, and in climbing that ladder she has no consideration for the moral values of a traditional Indian woman. She entangles herself in a number of extra-marital relations. Her love affair with the top hero Akshay Arora proves disastrous. Aasha Rani's life takes a drastic turn; from a simple innocent girl she changes into a fiery go-getter who shines in the Hindi film industry. She is a modern woman who carves an individuality for herself in the male-dominated Indian society. No matter how much scorn she receives from her less adventurous sisters for her degraded sinful life-style, she is a modern woman whom Shobha meticulously presents to the conservative tradition-conscious society.

In *Sisters*, Mikki and Alisha Hiralal are two half-sisters and legitimate heirs of the business tycoon Seth Hiralal. They try to make a place for themselves in the world of big business after the demise of their father. Mikki succeeds and becomes a business tycoon and in the process faces a number of challenges. At one point, to save her failing business empire she decides to tie up with another business tycoon Binny Malhotra. Mikki ends up marrying Binny on the advice of Amy: "The quickest way to shoot to the top is to tie up with Malhotra. A disastrous marriage can always be put behind you darling. These days divorce is not what it used to be. You are young and attractive. There will be a dozens of Malhotras later."[15]

Life according to these women is to be lived as they desire. They have money and power and anything else hardly matters. They hate men towering over them. They demand equality with them. When Mikki's relationship with her husband suffers because of his indifference to her wishes, she decides to walk out of the marriage. She sets up life afresh with her half-sister Alisha's love and support. They decide to face the world by themselves, as in the concluding part of the novel: "'To us,' Mikki toasted her sister, Alisha clinked her glass and echoed Mikki's words 'to us,' she said, adding wickedly, 'and to a great future—with or without man.'" (567)

Women of this new hyper-modern group care little for men. They consider men only a means to get to their desired ends. Unlike the traditional women who worship their men as their lords and masters, these new women drink, attend late night parties like men and refuse to remain at their mercy; rather they are out to teach men a lesson. The new woman is all set to turn the table upside down, and all notions of respectability and morality are sent crashing down the drain.

In De's *Strange Obsession*, the female protagonist Amrita Aggarwal, a young aspiring model, travels to Mumbai to carve a career in modelling. She messes up into an illicit relationship with a lesbian Meenakshi Aiyenger usually addressed as Minx. Minx starts following Amrita like a lover boy wherever she goes. She starts ruling her life. Minx encourages Amrita to indulge in sexual relation with her despite Amrita's strong objection. Minx forces her way and rebukes her for her recalcitrance: "Why? Why does it make you sick? Why should it? Because I belong to the same sex? Is that my only fault? You find it sickening to accept my love but what about that animal Rover's love? That's Okay. You enjoy that. How come? And don't tell 'because they are men and it's normal.' Bull shit! There is nothing abnormal about my feelings for you."[16]

Amrita is trapped in Minx's unnatural fascination and craze for her. Even after Amrita's getting married to Rakesh, Minx does not stop bothering her. This is an intense presentation of a woman falling for a woman instead of a man. Minx goes all out to revive Amrita's illicit relationship with her. She is just like a heart-broken lover when Amrita leaves her. It is hard to believe that a relationship of this type does happen in our modern society and it is only Shobha De's confidence which enables her to write this type of a novel in our still conservative society.

The lesbian relationship between Amrita and Minx shows the emerging reality of the new modern woman who finds sexual satisfaction with persons of the same gender. A new moral code is thus distinctly emerging, as these women freely choose their partners whether they belong to the opposite sex or to the same sex. Minx's behaviour toward Amrita is that of a protective lover and Amrita's slipping into this strange relationship is just another manifestation of the new woman's intriguing mentality which undermines the traditional notion of social acceptability of marriage or legitimate sexual relationship among persons of opposite sex.

In *Snapshots*, the women—Aparna, Swati, Reema, Surekha and Rashmi—are all modern women. They lead lives on their own terms. To them divorce is as normal as marriage. Aparna is a divorcee living on her own. She left her husband Rohit for she felt he did not live up to her standard. She starts an affair with Prem who works in her office. Previously her friend Swati had cheated her: Aparna caught Swati in a compromising position with her husband. After that incident Aparna is dead against Swati.

Swati comes back home after years in London and fixes a gathering of her old, close school friends at Reema's house. All her friends by this time are very much like her. They have become rich through their husbands. They all drink, have strings of lovers and are very independent, except for Noor who is a submissive Muslim woman left with little strength to assert herself. She is sexually exploited by her brother Nawaz. She had no qualms about it for she thought it was a normal thing to do and it was only Swati who made it clear to her that it was a most offensive thing to do, to have sexual relation with her own brother. When her conscience pricks, Noor commits suicide. But interpreted from the new woman's point of view she is a pessimist and a weak woman far different from her friends who are daredevils and believe in new morality of sexual promiscuity.

Swati is the most selfish of the group of friends in *Snapshots*. She is cunning and shrewd and most calculative among the six friends in the novel. By the end of their gathering at Reema's place she had done a most cruel thing. She had hidden a video tape camera to record all the conversations and events of the day as all the school friends gathered and talked about all the things they did as young girls.

They had gone to the extent of revealing even their sexual adventures and very personal matters. They had carried out even a strip tease show among themselves, which Swati had recorded. But Swati is caught red-handed when she is about to leave. She had carried out her cunning operation for she wanted to write, direct and produce a bold, T.V. series on the Indian urban woman of the Nineties. Swati's intention was not to malign her friends but to present a glamorous image of herself as a wanton actress and achieve fame by dazzling the viewers with a newly emerging glittering world of women. She had decided to come to India and collect some realistic material for her project and to her nothing was more appropriate and convenient than to organize a get together of her old school mates. In the women characters of this novel, De projects the image of the highly self-confident, self-reliant and fearless modern woman.

Shobha De's women do not care for any moral or traditional values. Again, in *Second Thoughts*, Maya, a young and ambitious Calcutta girl, marries a rich Mumbai businessman Ranjan and finds her relationship with her husband dry and mechanical.

Ranjan is an obedient Mama's boy and does everything with his mother's permission. Maya finds her role as a typical housewife very boring. Her husband, despite his high social position, is a typical Indian male who does not like women to work outside the home. Maya is bored beyond tolerance. Contrary to her expectation of finding her Bombay life after marriage full of fun, she finds it full of boredom. Her dream of a glamorous life remains unfulfilled. As Maya expresses her wish: "I wanted the city to seep into me slowly. I wanted to absorb it, digest it, make it a part of my system. I wanted desperately to become a Bombaywali. I wanted to belong."[17]

Ranjan taunts her when Maya once asks him to take her out at least during the weekend: "Sometimes you talk like such a kid. Life isn't a picnic, you know. And you are not in Bombay on a holiday. As a married woman, you have to learn to deal with responsibilities." (27)

Maya's frustration and her rebellious nature cannot allow her to take her husband's indifference lying down. Maya decides to seek the fulfillment of her dreams elsewhere, however sinful it might be. She starts taking a strong interest in her neighbour's young son Nikhil, a spoilt brat, who easily takes to Maya. Their affair becomes Maya's most precious enjoyment. She cleverly hides her affair from her workaholic husband. Of course, Maya gets nothing from her crazy relationship with Nikhil except sexual fulfillment. When Nikhil gets engaged with another girl she finds herself in a terrible situation. She is shocked and stunned and their relationship culminates at that point. Maya is left all alone once again with her mechanical husband and a towering mother-in-law. Her exploration of love and sex ends with Nikhil's exit from her life. Here, again, the traditional, morality-conscious and weak conservative Indian woman is left in an abject situation. Maya secretly enjoyed the forbidden fruit of promiscuity with her young neighbour. She got what she missed in her relationship with her husband, i.e. both companionship and sex but such a fulfillment was only temporary and short-lived. The real solution to her problem could not be found. The traditional woman suffered a serious disadvantage. In De's novels, the disadvantaged women break all those bonds and norms that delimit their freedom to fulfil their dreams or desires.

Women in De's novels want sexual pleasure outside their marriage. These women keep a dozen lovers. They want an identity outside the boundary of homes. They feel they are equal to men. They want their existence to be felt and recognized by all those they come in contact with. These women refuse to bow to tradition and convention and oppression. They are far from the conservative stronghold of Indian society. They have their own social circle; they care little for what their hostile critics in society may say. They do not care for anyone except themselves. They believe that the world is at their feet and sky is the limit for their progress and development. These are the new modern women, a very striking group that is emerging stealthily in Indian aristocratic society and which De presents in her novels with enthusiasm and creative energy.

Indian women over the centuries have been portrayed as pictures of pain, hardship and struggle. They have always been shown as dependants who live at the mercy of the men in their lives. They have no identity, dignity or individuality if they are made to stand a little farther from their men. Their life begins and ends in and around the house which is their permanent home from the very time they are married off by their parents. Liberty and individuality are unknown to them. Gradually with the advent of education from the West, the Indian society got a chance to see the advancement reached by the Western world and its liberal views toward women. It was not an easy task to make Indian men accept the fact that women were equally human like them. The gender bias always existed and even now at the dawn of the twenty-first century women still suffer however educationally enlightened they may be because it is always hard for the average Indian male to believe that women's demand for equal amount of liberty and rights enjoyed by men is just and justifiable. With the increasing awareness created by westernized education and the enlightened women using the women's liberation movement a new breed of young women sprouted in the conservative Indian society. Education opened the eyes of the simple urban and rustic Indian women. Women started coming out of their homes to experience and explore the outside world. This was not an easy task; a lot of hurdles and hardships had to be faced by them as they ventured to create some space for themselves in the fiercely hostile male-dominated Indian society.

Some women did succeed while a number of them failed. Women belonging to the middle and the higher middle class were more fortunate in this regard. They got a chance to explore a new world through educational enlightenment. It is they who started a new revolution for women's emancipation. A number of women writers came up with remarkable works advocating women's issues and looking at the world from a woman's perspective. Kamala Markandaya, Anita Desai, Nayantara Sahgal, Shashi Deshpande, Bharati Mukherjee, Arundhati Roy, Shobha De and others unreservedly expressed their views on the issues of women and society in their novels. Shobha De who joined this brigade in the late Nineties somehow managed to stand distinctly from all other women novelists of India. Her writings are marked by unreserved straightforward portrayals of a particular class of women who are filthy rich, powerful and reckless. She successfully discovers this new class of women who have started flourishing among the rich and mighty social strata. They form a small but significant portion of our huge population.

The new women aspire for everything that gives them extreme power and equal footing with their male counterparts. They are ready to make every compromise as long as they can get to their desired goal. There is a strong sense of individualism in them which makes them hard-to-suppress and hard-to-exploit partners of men. These women are all out to compete and excel in almost every field which was previously man's territory.

Socialite Evenings deals with women who represent the Indian high class. These women have money and status, rich powerful husbands and a string of devoted lovers. In *Socialite Evenings*, Karuna the female protagonist is a die-hard Mumbai socialite. Karuna marries for money. She leaves her husband as soon as she finds him incompatible. Her desire for freedom makes her change her life-style drastically. She becomes a reckless and self-absorbed woman with friends like Anjali and Ritu who have no regard for conventional moral values and whose sole motive is to achieve whatever they want. What Ranbir Roy remarks to Karuna on her flourishing career in advertising and refusal to marry him is indeed significant: 'Anyway—cut to you as you are now—disgustingly self-assured and revoltingly self-sufficient. Baby—you'll give one of those padded shouldered Wall Street American boards a run for their money. This is going to be a terrific project . . . get your half-baked views on dowry deaths—perhaps coerce into saying stuff the American media will lap up—like your refusal to remarry since you don't want to end up as a heap of kerosened ashes." (223)

Aasha Rani in *Starry Nights* rises to superstardom using some of the most revolting techniques and tricks to reach star status. She sells her body in trying to have a firm feet in the Hindi film industry. It is not only Aasha Rani but a good number of other heroines who have made a place for themselves using their body as the main bait to get what they aspire for. Women in the glamour world are, in traditional parlance, characterless with no consideration for traditional morality which, in fact, is called into question. Knowing well this fact, the new generation of ambitious women is ready to make every compromise as long as they can get riches and fame. There is a craze among the new generation girls. Once they realize that they have alluring physical assets they look for grabbing a place for themselves in the tinsel glamour world of Mumbai. These women are well aware of the price they have to pay to reach the land of their heart's desire. Their high-profile ambitions make them overlook the dirty side of the film world. Aasha Rani uses her body to get the roles she wants to do. She goes to bed with the film director Jojo to seek acceptance of her preferences:

> "Why don't I play the other woman?" She suggested brightly. "Why don't you adapt your script a little so that she's not a teen-ager. I don't mind doing a negative role provided it's young." (365)

Aasha Rani doesn't hesitate to use her body as a bait to get favour from Jojo in getting the role she wants. She symbolizes the modern woman who uses everything in her power to achieve what she covets even if it requires going to bed with the man who can fulfil her desires.

In *Sisters*, there are two leading female characters Alisha and Mikki Hiralal, daughters of the same father but different mothers, who are in a stiff competition to make a place for themselves in the tough world of big business. Both the women leave no stone unturned to reach the topmost positions in this highly competitive field. Mikki, in her bid to save her business empire, marries another business tycoon Binny who turns out to be a cheat. Mikki suffers in marriage. But Alisha prospers in her business. Later she comes to her sister Mikki's rescue despite their initial enmity as half-sisters. They decide to face the world together as sisters. In these two women De gives a true picture of the fiercely ambitious modern new woman.

The new woman has so much liberty that she even sets up a new home away from home in pursuance of her career. This is seen in the case of Amrita in *Strange Obsession*, who goes all by herself from Delhi to Mumbai to pursue a career in modelling and make money. Amrita faces sexual abuse from Minx and even submits to it, though she slowly begins to enjoy this new experience, as she starts adapting it as a part of her existence in Mumbai. Despite her strong initial rejection of it Minx's lesbianism becomes Amrita's delight.

Amrita's staying away from home and staying alone in Mumbai for her modelling career shows how much goal-oriented and individualistic she is. She is so happy with her modelling career and the fame she gets from it that she does not allow her unnatural sexual relationship with Minx to become a hindrance.

De's women in the novels that followed *Socialite Evenings—Sultry Days*, *Snapshots* and *Second Thoughts*—show a continuation of similar behavioural traits of the new woman. They are all daring women and have lots of stamina to face the stress and strain of the high society they live in. They are not afraid of facing every brick thrown in their way in their endeavour to lead lives on their own terms. Power, money and fame are the three biggest aspirations of the new women. They are ready to take up every challenge which lies before them to get what they want. Nothing matters to them as long as they can enjoy life. They refuse to look on man as their superior. They are daring lionesses on the prowl, out to attack everything that comes to hinder them from catching their prey. This is the new image of the modern woman which De daringly brings out in all her novels.

NOTES

1. Anil Kumar Singh, "Women in Indo-Anglian Fiction: A Concentrated Study of Major Cases in Point," Unpublished doctoral dissertation, Manipur University, 1993, p. 57.
2. *Ibid.*, pp. 66-67.
3. Raja Rao, *The Serpent and the Rope* (New Delhi, 1968), p. 235.
4. R.K. Narayan, *The Guide* (Mysore, 1978), p. 201.
5. K. Meera Bai, "Tradition and Modernity: The Portrayal of Women by Women Writers," *Indian Women Novelists*, ed. R.K. Dhawan (New Delhi: Prestige, 1991), p. 35.
6. *Loc. cit.*
7. Kamala Markandaya, *Nectar in a Sieve* (Bombay, 1980), p. 113.
8. Kamala Markandaya, *A Silence of Desire* (London, 1960), p. 7.

9. Chaman Nahal, "Feminism in Indian English Fiction," *Indian Women Novelists*, ed. R.K. Dhawan, Vol. I, p. 38.
10. Kamala Markandaya, *A Handful of Rice* (London, 1960), p. 7.
11. B.P. Sinha, "Nayantara Sahgal's Novels," *The Quest*, Vol. II, No. 2 (Ranchi, 1997), p.33.
12. Arundhati Roy, *The God of Small Things* (New Delhi, 1997), p. 47.
13. Shobha De, *Socialite Evenings*, in *Shobha De Omnibus* (New Delhi, 1995), p. 44.
14. Shobha De, *Starry Nights*, in *Shobha De Omnibus*, p. 236.
15. Shobha De, *Sisters*, in *Shobha De Omnibus*, p 468.
16. Shobha De, *Strange Obsession*, in *Shobha De Omnibus*, p. 596.
17. Shobha De, *Second Thoughts* (New Delhi, 1996), p. 27.

Aesthetics and Morality: Emergence of the New Woman

Aesthetics is concerned with beauty and art and the understanding of beautiful things.[1] Hence the appeal to human eyes, mind and spirit are the basic objectives of aesthetics in writing a book or in any work of art. Shobha De has come up with her own aesthetic approach in her novels. Her aesthetics lies in her ability to bring out human values in her writings. Her talent also lies in her catchy, blunt and candid writings which hit the human heart and mind directly. Her novels represent the woman's challenge to the patriarchal society, that is, women are no longer doormats to be trode upon and dirtied. Her women no longer submit to the age-old traditional values and social practices. De is tireless and unhindered in depicting the life-styles of the rich society aristocrats in general and the women in particular. Though blunt and undecorative in her presentations, her aesthetics consists in her sincerity in bringing out the quite different character and values of the new woman whom she ceaselessly portrays in almost all her novels. This woman is highly individualistic, calculative and self-centred. In fact every woman character in her novels shows extreme independence and recklessness. There is nothing poetic or decorative about De's realistic writing. She writes freely, using sexually explicit words without any fear of disapproval from the average conservative Indian reading public. She writes unhindered and unmindful of the hostile criticism of her novels generally regarded as obscene and pornographic. But the educated middle class women admire her for her boldness to cut across the conservative morality. "She has completely changed the idea of literature by increasing interest in English pulp fiction" says C.P. Surendran, a poet-journalist.[2]

Socialite Evenings, De's maiden novel and the first to explore the lives of the wealthy urban Indians, was a sensation as the novel threw open to a wide view a much-closed subject of sexual promiscuity. The novel projected a new breed of women who demand equality with men in all walks of life. The novel won acclaim from the upcoming breed of the whole new generation of educated, motivated and assertive urban women. Shobha De's work became an instant hit with her outrageous and daring revelation of the Mumbai high society with all its glamour and dirt.

Controversy came in torrents when De's second novel *Starry Nights* hit the bookstands in 1991. Many of the male members of Mumbai's high society felt outraged. The novel, set in the city's film industry, is packed with unsavoury characters based on real life tycoons and film producers. Reviewers, mostly male, trashed the book as low brow, but the public by and large loved it. "Porn again De," declared one headline. "Queen of Quickies," cried another. That year, an international magazine dubbed De as "the Jackie Collins of India" which certainly gave a big leap to increasing her readership outside India.[3]

A series of novels followed the first two: *Sisters* and *Strange Obsession* came in 1992, *Sultry Days* in 1994, *Snapshots* in 1995 and *Second Thoughts* in 1996. The popularity of De's novels rose due to their contents. She was recognized as a master storyteller and an expert in using the appropriate language. Her novels testify to her intimate understanding of the psyche of women and their problems.

Readers and critics have reacted variously to De's writing. Her fictional world has aroused curiosity and interest. It has invited her downright rejection and denunciation because of the unrestricted depiction of sexual details of the life of the rich and powerful members of the upper class society in India.

However, while De presents these titillating details, her pointer is toward the arrival of the new Indian woman on the social scene who is eager to defy the orthodox system of Indian society and break its age-old value system oriented toward the strengthening of male domination over the female. De's novels are not just a series of body-showing stories. According to David Davidar, they are serious attempts at "discovering India through Indian eyes."[4]

De has created characters in tune with the themes she deals with. Her chief purpose seems to be to call attention to the kind of treatment meted out to women in India. She does not present these women's social situation for any idealistic purpose or aesthetic effect. But there is an aesthetic flavour too in her writing and in her presentation of the women characters which gives De a prominent place among the new generation of Indian-English writers. This is indeed a positive achievement.

As Shobha De's women present a new pattern of values, a new set of values has come into light with the coming of this new breed of women who are independent and assertive. The traditional moral values have undergone a total change. Manifesting their new pattern of values, these women characters may be perceived and regarded as characterless women by the majority of members of the Indian society. But the fact of the matter is that this society is itself in a state of transition. It has not yet given up the traditional values nor has it accorded recognition to the new values of the post-Independence Indian society which has emerged with its own set of moral and aesthetic values.

According to *Oxford Advanced Learner's Dictionary*, Morals means to be concerned with principles of right and wrong behaviour.[5] Morality in a way is the sum total of values of people at a particular time. Novel or fiction as a form of art, deeply concerned with society, reflects the value system of an age.[6] They are written keeping in mind the accepted social values and norms which in short constitute the morals of the society.

That is the reason why Indian writers in English find it difficult to write freely without regard to social moral values. "Hesitations surround each move and aspect of it. This may be attributed to the typical nature of the Indian middle class to which the writer belongs."[7]

Noted women novelists of India such as Anita Desai and Nayantara Sahgal have presented their respective images of the new modern woman adhering to new morality of the time in their novels.

Nayantara Sahgal's women and their morality are somewhat similar to Shobha De's though De's women display an element of greater aggressiveness and daring in their deportment. Anita Desai's women are no doubt modern women but they stick to the old values despite their realization that they need to break free from the old moral shackles which bind them. Their mode of rebellion is to commit suicide.

Nayantara Sahgal comes close to Shobha De in strongly protesting the denial of freedom to Indian woman. She believes in "New Humanism" and "New Morality" according to which the woman is not to be taken as a "sex object and a glamour doll, fed on fake dreams of perpetual youth, lulled into a passive role that requires no individual identity."[8] In her novels she pleads for new marital morality based on mutual trust, consideration, generosity and absence of pretence, selfishness and self-centredness. The new morality based on freedom from fear, frank communication and mutual love can, according to Sahgal, 'create the "oxygen of understanding" which can save the present generation from the explosive psychic trauma of marital conflict.'[9]

Sahgal's novels *This Time of Morning* (1965), *Storm in Chandigarh* (1969) and *The Day in Shadow* (1971) portray women believing in and practising new morality. Though they enjoy high status as wives of rich businessmen or diplomats yet they yearn for individual freedom. They are dejected and angry in their marital relationships. Sahgal's heroines, Rashmi, Saroj and Simrit, contemplate divorce as the ultimate means to overcome their unhappiness. Divorce actually happens in *The Day in Shadow* and with it the troubles of being single come to Simrit weighing her down both physically and financially. But she experiences the feeling of freedom in her as she administers the shock of separation to her irresponsible and care-free husband who had taken her for granted and could never imagine that she could take such a path-breaking step.

The aesthetic values of Sahgal's women too consist in realizing their dreams of freedom and individuality cherished by Indians before achieving independence. Freedom and individuality is what the heroines of Sahgal's novels seek even though they are bound by the culture and traditional practices of the conservative Indian society. Like Simrit who lashes out fearlessly: "I hate this century except for the freedom it brought for countries and people, especially for women. But it is barbaric otherwise, full of rotten, elastic standards and the worship of money. I hate the whole mess of human affairs."[10]

Sahgal's women characters live an intensely passionate life—a life free from all inhibitions and taboos. According to her, Saroj's premarital sex has nothing to do with the pollution of flesh, promiscuity or immorality. She wants women to break off from the orthodox rules and conventions that make people fearful of each other. She seems to be searching for a place where there will be no hindrance and suffering in seeking individual freedom. She is liberal in her views on marriage, divorce and love. These views point to the new morality coming up and social changes taking place as a result of change occurring deep inside the individual, which the writer tries to express in her works. This new female awakening is seen in Sahgal's novels and is also taken up by Shobha De in a more daring and explosive form as she seems to become more and more concerned with the portrayal of the new woman's dreams and aspirations in her work.

Another woman novelist who writes about the changing morality in the society is Anita Desai. She focuses on the women's inner world, her sensibility and her frustration at being born a woman in a male-dominated society. Her women are anguished and tired of the illusory quality of all human relationships. They also evince their rejection of the traditional role cut out for women by society. In her novel *Cry, the Peacock*, Maya the protagonist is a young and beautiful woman brought up under the guidance of a doting father. Maya suffers a loveless marriage with Gautama. Nearly always preoccupied with his office works as a lawyer he can hardly visualize Maya's loneliness and her need for the physical companionship of her husband.

Like the peacock, Maya loves intensely but her love is totally unreciprocated. When Maya passionately craves for Gautama's love he flees the scene. As a result Maya loses all interest in the things outside herself. She lapses into a psychotic condition. She becomes insane and wants to kill Gautama for not reciprocating her love. She condemns Gautama to death. Overwhelmed by her sense of guilt and self-hatred she kills herself too. The violent act of killing her husband transforms Maya from the meek traditional suffering wife into a self-assertive and destructively daring modern woman.

Again, in *Voices in the City*, the female protagonist Monisha finds her marriage to Jiban a misfortune. Like Maya, Monisha feels desperately lonely and lost in this marriage. Jiban turns out to be a cold, unfeeling husband. Monisha's yearning for a little privacy is shattered by her living in the joint family. She feels deprived of her sense of individuality and respectability. She has to depend on her husband for everything. The incident of Monisha's taking a few rupees from the cupboard without her husband's permission highlights an Indian woman's economic dependence—a sort of soul-destroying parasitic existence where the wife has to seek permission for paying her brother's hospital bill.

Monisha's suffering throws light on the sad plight of the educated unemployed Indian women of our times. Her suicide is the result of a desperate wish to be free of all such shabby relationships in which the woman has to stoop so low. Anita Desai's women have no clear perception of a beautiful life they ought to live. They are suicidal by nature; they become victims rather than ambitious, self-assertive planners of a beautiful future.

In *Where Shall We Go This Summer?*, Anita Desai projects the loneliness of the female protagonist Sita. Sita is bound both by family and society. She finds her fifth pregnancy after her four children unwanted. Yet, she is confused as to what to do with the baby developing in her womb. She does not want to bear it nor is she ready for an abortion. Her children and family are indifferent to her mental suffering and there is no one, not even her husband, to understand her plight. She leaves Bombay in terror. Leaving her husband Raman in despair, she travels to Manori island in desperation, "in order to achieve the miracle of not giving birth."[11] But Shobha De's female protagonists crave for loneliness; they believe that in that state of being single they can experience independence and live life on their own terms. Their loneliness is a part of their perception of living a beautiful life, alone and independently.

Sita seems to be made to think this way to assert her individuality. Notwithstanding these thoughts, she finally returns to her husband after realizing that she might better show patience and courage to face life with all its hardships.

Anita Desai's women in the first two novels are tired of the existing social conditions which makes their lives meaningless and hence not worth living. They suffer from a sense of alienation and loss of identity which is expressed in their neurotic outbursts and self-annihilation. This happens because the women though conscious of their suffering cannot take up any daring reformative steps to ameliorate their tragic situations caused by their adherence to social and family values. They are rather weak and self-destructive. Maya and Monisha see no other way to get out of the vicious circle and commit suicide. In the third novel Desai comes out with another image of woman who is intelligent and sensitive. Sita's initial revolt and later her returning to her family shows her timidity. But it also shows her sensitivity to the difficult situation she is in. As such, Anita Desai's women do not belong to the class of the new women; a deeper analysis of their character reveals that nearly all of them conform to traditional social life. Despite their sensitiveness and realization of the evils of society, there is hardly anyone who possesses those attributes that would qualify her to be regarded as the new woman. Shobha De has a definite edge over Desai in shaping the image of the new woman in her novels. Her portrayal of the new woman is remarkably different from Anita Desai's portrayal and quite in tune with the spirit of the feminist movement.

Shobha De's novels present a totally new concept of morality. She elaborately dwells upon the much covertly discussed theme of sex in her novels. She presents women who defy social conventions and choose to lead their lives on their own terms. But in a country like India, women however educated they may be have to act keeping in mind that they are bound by traditional values and social acceptability. De's women are totally different; they represent a small but significant section of Indian society which is gradually changing its outlook with the changing times. They are women who seek equal rights with men. They don't want to be placed second to men. They seek friendship with men who can give them unending supply of luxury, money and comfort. These women marry for convenience and their living singly does not worry them. They engage themselves in glamorous and challenging careers like modelling, acting, journalism, designing, advertising and even big business. To the common conservative middle-class Indian, this sort of highflying life-style is very unwelcome and not in keeping with womanly behaviour and life-style. Women belonging to this class are considered too modern and sophisticated, westernized and, above all, characterless. The protagonists of De's novels exhibit this trait in their character.

Karuna in *Socialite Evenings* hails from a conservative middle class family and plunges in the circle of Mumbai high society after her bureaucrat father's posting in this glittering city. She leaves her middle class values and moral standards and embraces the high life of the rich upper class. Her modelling career which she opts for much against her father's wishes is the first step she takes to become a part of the glamour world. Her meeting with Anjali, a prominent socialite and the wife of a wealthy playboy, makes Karuna's entry into the high society easier. She marries for money, little considering her incompatibility with her husband. Later she finds that she had made a mistake in choosing her husband because the man turns out to be just an average Indian, unexciting and uninspiring. Compared with the outgoing and fun-loving Karuna, her husband proves a dull partner. Impelled by her desire for fun and excitement, she cheats her husband and plans for a holiday with her lover Krish: "While he was innocently instructing me, I was already planning, when and how I'd meet Krish. At the airport? Hotel? What we'd do together—how liberated and free we'd feel without any pressures on us."[12]

Marriage is considered a game for security and convenience. If the wife is not happy with her husband, she can pack up and go away any moment. Unlike Anjali, Karuna never takes her marriage seriously. Yet both of them get divorced. Divorce is not an easy thing in the Indian conservative set up and it only happens when the husband is unbearably cruel. A wife's place is at her husband's house. But all of Shobha De's women—in *Socialite Evenings*, *Starry Nights*, *Sisters*, *Sultry*

Days, *Strange Obsession*, *Snapshots* and *Second Thoughts*—reveal that they care two hoots for social disapproval and listen only to the yearnings of their hearts. For them man is just a means to an end. These women look for their personal satisfaction in everything they do. They refuse to be passive followers of their husbands' dictates. This is contrary to the traditional moral outlook of Indian society where a woman, who has male friends, or drinks and smokes, or wears revealing clothes and indulges in socially unacceptable relationships, is considered immoral. But these new fashion-loving or behavioral traits have come into the life of the Indian woman from the western society. While some of these traits may be somewhat tolerated, too much of westernization in the atmosphere of Indian society is still looked upon with disdain and suspicion. This is because the traditional image of woman still lurks in the minds of people. The educated woman is beset with the problem of striking an acceptable compromise between modern thinking and aesthetic perceptions and the traditional morality which dogs her at every step.

The standard of morality in De's women has emerged out of women's' excessive exposure to westernized education, wealth, power and fame. This new morality has changed the face of the new woman who is slowly raising her head in the fast advancing Indian civilization. With the rise of the new woman, nearly every middle class educated woman aspires for more comfort, more wealth and more independence. Given a chance to have a break in any lucrative high-flying career any new generation Indian woman would jump at the opportunity, no matter what amount of compromise they have to make on the home front. The younger generation of women is ready to grab such opportunities and experience the sensation of being in the high social circle which appears so tempting. It happens with both Karuna and Anjali. Both had a middle class upbringing but it is only after taking up new careers—one as a model and the other as an air hostess—and getting married to rich businessmen that these two women enter the awesome world of fame and wealth.

Aasha Rani in *Starry Nights* sleeps with prominent men in the film industry to get herself a plum role and place herself firmly in the dirty world of Hindi show business. However there is a little difference in her case as the new woman. It is her mother who pushes her into this glittering yet shady world. Her mother takes her from one producer to another making her wear dazzling outfits. Before stepping into the Mumbai film industry, her mother had exposed her to the dirty world of B-grade films: "She'd forced Aasha Rani to perform in blue films. When she was not quite twelve, there was only one thing in her mind. To save enough money to get Viji to Bombay."[13]

Amma's dream of making her daughter a big film star in Mumbai makes her tread paths she had not herself trodden. She impels Aasha Rani to go to bed with the well-known men in the film industry in order to bag a lead role in Hindi films. She thus turns a blind eye to her daughter's unwillingness. For instance:

> Kishenbhai had come over swiftly to Aasha Rani's side and said softly, 'M.D. has a room upstairs—go with him. He will feed you. M.D. is an important man. Treat him nicely. He can help your career. Don't create a scene or anything. All you have to do is . . . is . . . what you do with me . . . bas. It will be OK. Tomorrow morning I will come and take you home.' Aasha Rani had pleaded with her eyes and looked beseechingly at Amma—who'd simply averted hers. (247)

There have been comments on the character of Aasha Rani by the public. "Many people also wanted to know if the heroine was modelled on Rekha, a Bollywood siren from Southern India. De's answer was that she could have used virtually any Southern actress in Bombay because they all end up in unconventional relationship."[14]

The world of Bombay Hindi film industry is known to be full of hungry wolves. As such new talents and aspirants entering the industry as actresses face difficult situations. The ritual of undergoing a tryst with the big names selecting the cast for a movie seems to be the operating key. *Starry Nights* shows the strange morals of these persons who shine in the film industry. Married men flirt openly with the newly inducted actresses. Likewise, the wives get used to their husbands' wild philandering and feel free to flirt with the menfolk they like. There is no consideration for marital conventions. Aasha Rani freely sleeps with her co-star Akshay Arora who is a much-married man. She even contemplates marriage with him though Akshay firmly declines the proposal. Akshay's refusal makes Aasha Rani swallow an overdose of pills and attempt suicide. Women seem to care little about the consequences of their crazy acts. It seems absolutely normal for both husband and wife or for lovers to make or break any number of illicit relationships. The body becomes only a mechanism to get their wishes fulfilled both physically as well as monetarily. The lives of these women despite their fame and success are not always fun and frolic. They become tense and anxiety-ridden owing to the futility of the wild lives they lead.

The moral lives of the modern woman can be yet again visualized from Shobha De's *Sisters*. In this novel, the two half sisters, Mikki and Alisha Hiralal, are neck deep in competition trying to outdo each other in business rivalry. They become assertive and highly independent. The two sisters remain isolated from each other as their father due to his promiscuity had them from different women. Mikki is the daughter of the properly wedded wife and Alisha the product of his illicit passion for a whore. Alisha is hostile and bitter to Mikki who had enjoyed all the comforts as Hiralal's legitimate daughter right from her childhood while she is deprived of these comforts because her true identity is concealed which gives the impression of her being an illegitimate child.

They are busy young women trying to carry on the legacy of their illustrious industrialist dead father. For these women life is a never-ending strife for perfection. They are hungry for the best in every field. In the beginning Alisha competes with Mikki in everything—even in seeking boy friends. Navin is their common boy friend. Alisha is devastated when Navin prefers Mikki to her. Mikki makes a shrewd move as she leaves her fiancé Navin despite a lot of society talk that they were engaged. Marriages are viewed as commercial affairs. A husband has to be one who can be of some use to his wife, and Navin just does not fit into her picture of the husband she looks for. She needs someone who can help her anchor the sinking Hiralal empire. She knows that Binny Malhotra will make a smart husband and hence prove suitable for the role she has for him. Binny's charming way makes Mikki fall totally under his spell. Binny too has his reasons for marrying Mikki: "He had money, power and access to anybody he wanted to meet in the government. The only thing he didn't have was acceptability in society. It was the one thing Binny craved for more than anything else. And no one was going to deny him the status of being Mallika Hiralal's husband—and the owner of Hiralal Industries."[15]

Mikki marries him but she is shattered when she finds that Binny has a mistress Malini who has two children. Binny turns out to be a dominating husband, putting a complete stop to Mikki's career as a businesswoman. He does not want her to be working outside home but just to sit pretty at home. When Mikki expresses her desire to go to office, Binny gives her an unpleasant reply: "Listen very carefully, princess. This is no longer your father's home and you are no longer the pampered child. You are Binny Malhotra's wife. And you'd better start behaving like her. In our family women are trained to obey their husbands. Your job is to look beautiful. I told you that when I married you. Buy clothes. Buy jewellery. Go to the beauty parlour. Play bridge. Learn golf. Attend cooking classes that's all. But no questions—you don't have the right." (491)

Mikki becomes a slave. She has to part with all her freedom and yet she does all this in her blind love for Binny. The final blow comes when Mikki is thrown out by Binny. Mikki takes shelter in her cousin Shanay's arms and later seeks Alisha's support, approaching her as an elder loving sister. Being sensible women they know that their friendship matters more than a thousand Navins. They decide to meet every challenge with their joint effort. These are women who despite the hurdles in their way resolve to be independent and they achieve their purpose sooner or later. This image of the new woman surmounting all obstacles in her way keeps emerging in De's novels.

Amrita in *Strange Obsession* is another challenging woman who travels all alone from Delhi to Mumbai to pursue a career in modelling. She goes through a lot of turmoils as she messes up with the lesbian Minx who becomes her constant companion. Minx is obsessively crazy for Amrita and they begin having a sexual relationship, though it is much against Amrita's will. Amrita despite her earlier unwillingness submits to Minx's amorous advances: "Amrita lay back against the pillow inertly. Her mind switched into a dream-like state. She shut her eyes and ceased to think or feel, surrendering to Minx who was over her, moving her hands tenderly . . . caressing her face, kissing her softly. She felt Minx's finger . . . and she did not resist."[16] Amrita in fact starts responding to the crazy love of Minx. As she admits to Minx's father: "I began to enjoy it. To respond in fact, it is a neutral response from both." (699)

Amrita goes close to Minx as the latter fulfils most of her needs—a good house and somebody taking care of her finances. The only thing she is unable to get from their relationship is a child. Amrita's marriage to Rakesh finally saves her from this crazy relationship. The new woman's seeking for fulfillment even within her own sex is seen clearly in the women of De. These women show a desire to prove that they may not need to depend on man's company.

Women to women sexual relations or what is called lesbianism have been increasing in the conservative Indian society despite the society's lack of recognition to this practice. This sort of relationship is more prominently seen among the upper rich classes. At present time the increase in lesbianism may be due to the revolt of women against the society and its norms which underrate women. This itself is another feature of the new woman in Shobha De's novels.

Shobha De's women go all out in enjoying the status as the new modern woman. They shatter the age-old concept of the traditional Indian woman with their assertive, individualistic and carefree attitude towards life. In this new image the new women have got extreme independence in almost every field and one of the most striking and interesting freedoms they enjoy is sexual freedom. No longer is the new woman dependent on man for her sexual fulfillment. A new sexual practice is adopted by De's women, i.e., lesbianism, which means sexual relationship between women. It would be worthwhile to examine the historical background of this strange yet well-known relationship from ancient times. In the *Kamasutra*, the famous classic of Hindu erotica, there is a clear mention of lesbianism:

> Some women of the harem
> When they are amorous
> Do the acts of the mouth congress
> On the yonis of one another.
>
> (Vatsyayan, *Kamasutra*, XIV)[17]

The sexually-starved inmates of the harem contrived to attain sexual gratification through the daughters of a muse, a woman friend or a maidservant, who dressed and acted like a male, by penetrating a root or a fruit, resembling a male organ fastened to the front part of her waist. In another treatise on statecraft and penology, *Manusmriti*, punishment is given for spoiling a young girl through lesbian contact, mutual sexual gratification:

> If an unmarried girl spoiled another raw girl and taught her the lesson of self-abuse or gratified with her fingers or other counterfeit male organ or cylindrical substances she was liable to pay fine of two hundred currency coins. Besides the fine she was to subsidize the parents of the deflorated girl with double the amount of the calculated dowry and also to receive ten lashes. But if a married woman exercised similar grit she was to be awarded a more merciless punishment. Her head was shaved, her fingers were excised and she was paraded in the public streets on the back of a donkey. (*Manusmirti*, VIII, 369-70)[18]

The word lesbianism is derived from the Greek Lesbios, a Greek island in the Aegean sea which was the native place of Sappho, the 7th Century B.C. lyric poetess who addressed her love poems to women.[19]

Lesbianism hence is a universal phenomenon where women find sexual fulfillment among themselves. Writers have known and written about it. Here is an example from a late nineteenth century French novel *Aphrodrite* by Prierre Louys: "A woman is a perfect instrument. From head to toe she's made solely and wonderfully for love. Only a woman knows how to be loved. Therefore, if a couple is composed of two women, it's perfect; if it has only one woman, it's only half as good; if it has no women at all, it's completely idiotic."[20]

A similar preference of woman is expressed in the following poem:

> My source of happiness is a soft skinned girl . . .
> The moisture of her mouth is sweet and fresh to those who care to taste.
> Between her legs a fissure lies as pretty and alluring as the neck of some gazelle.

> And when her beauty was first laid bare to me I said what I felt in my heart:
> "Praise be to Him who has moulded such beauty . . .
> My night was one of sucking at her mouth and throat,
> And if to love a girl in such a way is sinful, to love a man's unlawful.[21]

This preference is also because of different kinds of psychic rapport between women not to be found in heterosexual relationship in which a woman's role is inferior. She is rode over by the male. She is made love to, not made love with.[22]

Even in the present time lesbianism is considered sinful and a taboo subject by the society. Yet, it cannot be totally rejected as sinful or distasteful for a section of women by their own psychological set up cannot follow the normal pattern of sexual relationship between a man and a woman. They have an inborn quality of liking the same sex both physically as well as mentally. In another case, due to strong hatred or rejection of men's domination and superiority in the society or having received no love and understanding in the surroundings in which they live, women by their psychological and biological needs are inclined to take to lesbianism.

A majority of women, both lesbian and heterosexual, are taught that their sexuality must conform to certain modes of behavior. The society with its existent culture voices shame upon a woman if she goes beyond the criteria of passivity and repression, and doubts her virtue if she refuses. A woman is taught to suppress sexual desires and needs by conceding all pleasure to the male; even talking about participation and satisfaction in sex is taboo. So most women learn to hate their bodies and usually possess little knowledge of their bodies and their reproductive systems or their physiology.[23]

It is true that inability of a woman to realize her own worth made her inferior to man all the time. A woman even in our times never had given so much of thought to her sexual behaviour nor ever realized how far she has had an equal amount of participation or willingness in her sexual relationship with a man. Not infrequently she had displayed the image of the weak, shy, traditional woman who feels it was an unwomanly behaviour to express her desires regarding this much covered and secretly discussed topic of sex. Shobha De shatters this image of the traditional woman in her novels and presents the daring, non-conformist and highly self-confident image of the new woman. She gives so much of independence to her main women characters that they show up as admirably strong and highly intriguing persons who challenge male hegemony fearlessly. And it is interesting and at the same time awesome to see women seeking sexual relationship with women without bothering for any social sanction. This sort of lesbian relationship is given a clear focus in some of her novels namely, *Starry Nights* and *Strange Obsession*.

In *Starry Nights*, the much talked about novel which deals with Mumbai film world is full of sexual orgies of the attractive, super rich film personalities. Almost every conceivable and non-conceivable form of sexual behaviour is presented in the novel. Besides heterosexual behaviour she has presented the most awesome and intriguing sexual relationship i.e., the woman to woman relationship. This form of sexual behaviour and its implication to the new woman is another main topic of discussion in this chapter.

The protagonist of *Starry Nights*, Aasha Rani, shares a passionate relationship with her journalist friend Linda. But before she comes across Linda she had experienced lesbian pleasure when she had gone to Dubai through a ticket from Seth Amirchand. In Dubai she was given every comfort by her host, a gold smuggler who was not interested in sleeping with her. But she had sexual fulfillment to the full as she was attended upon by two Thai masseurs from Bangkok which was her first experience of and exposure to lesbian pleasure:

> She got her shopping done, plus she had her body dexterously worked over by the Thai girls, who giggled at the size of Aasha Rani's breasts (like melons) and took turns rubbing coconut oil

> over them. Aasha Rani found their ministrations most pleasurable and thought of Akshay and how unpleasant. . . . The Thai girls asked her flirtatiously whether she wanted to try a 'sandwich massage.' Game to try anything once, Aasha Rani agreed readily.
>
> It was an experience so sensuous, so arousing, so complete, that it was weeks before she could forget the feel of two, smooth, soft oiled, practically breastless bodies on either side of her, touching, tickling, stroking every naked inch, making her skin tingle and come alive in a way she couldn't have imagined possible.
>
> When she returned to Bombay . . . she had experienced some of the greatest orgasms of her life. (277)

Aasha Rani has this experience deeply embedded in her mind forever as she describes the greatest orgasm which she derived in the expert hands of the Thai girls.

Later, Aasha Rani experiences her second lesbian relation which is presented at great length in the novel:

> "Come here," she said to Aasha Rani, "Take a sip, come on, yaar, let's enjoy ourselves. . . . With that she pulled Aasha Rani down on the bed and kissed her on the lips.
>
> It was a pleasant feeling, Aasha Rani thought. No rough bristles scraping her face, just smooth cheeks and soft lips over her own. A memory flashed in her head of the Thai masseuses. Linda's hands were in Aasha Rani's hair, expertly undoing the clasp. . . . Her fingers began messaging her neck as once again she bent over to kiss her saying, "Open your mouth let me taste your tongue. Your tongue looked so sexy and pink—relax, baby relax. You will love it. Just leave it all to me. Trust me."
>
> . . . "This is love, understand? This is love making, not what those bastards do to our bodies." Aasha Rani was lulled to sleep by Linda's fingers stroking her. Yes, she thought, this is what it should be, tender, beautiful and erotic. In a way it could never happen with a man. (287-88)

What Aasha Rani finally concludes after this sexual experience was that, what she and Linda shared was completely normal and rightful. She had several sexual experiences with men but they were always one-sided. She only offered her body to those men and they had used her body thinking only of their own pleasure and caring little or not at all about what she must be feeling by their wild, brutal assaulting type of sexual behaviour. Aasha Rani never enjoyed those experiences. She only had done it automatically almost like a daily choir. With Linda, she had experienced full pleasure and complete ecstasy. She felt nothing dirty about the fact that she was having sex with someone from her own sex. She loved it and felt greatly satisfied. This feeling of hers personifies another quality of the image of the new woman who wants everything she experiences to be worthwhile and satisfactory. What Linda and Aasha Rani did was nothing unnatural to the new type of woman who feels that sex with a woman is much more satisfying than with man who leaves her all hurt and dirty after having satisfied himself with hardly a second thought whether the woman had enjoyed the act or not. So lesbianism is also a part of the revolting spirit inside the new woman. They seem to be all out to satisfy every female urge and wish even if it be the sexual one to be fulfilled within their own sex.

Again, in De's *Strange Obsession*, the entire story revolves around lesbianism with the two leading characters i.e. Amrita and Minx sharing this highly resentful relationship. Meenakshi Iyengar (Minx) had a disturbed childhood and had only her busy police officer father looking after her. Minx yearned for her mother's love but she failed to receive any. All her growing up years were spent with her father. It had a psychotic impact on her for she had started liking her father sexually. She developed an unnatural attraction towards him. She rather pities her father of his sexless life. She even starts imagining herself having sex with him. She confesses that she had also developed a feeling of hatred for men from childhood as a result of inhuman beatings she got from her father. This had made her into a revolutionary who now hates everything associated with men and turned her into a lesbian.

She had distanced herself from society as she had grown up without any friends. She had become a psychologically sick person. She had left school and fallen into bad company becoming friendly with the local dadas. Subsequently she develops hatred for her father and every man. She becomes a lesbian and forces a lesbian relationship on the upcoming model Amrita.

Minx becomes a crazy obsessed lover of Amrita. She confesses that she is ready to do anything for her:

> What more do I have to do to prove myself? Kill? I'll do that too. Just tell me—who? You want me to kill someone? Anyone? I'll do it. I'll kill for you. I will Amrita . . . maybe then you'll love me. . . Will that make you happy? Will that please you? Then I'll do it—just tell me to, and I'll do it. I'll kill myself. I'll give you my life—What more can I give you? (607-8)

True to her word, Minx kills Lola, a rival to Amrita in their modelling world. She attacks her with acid and brutally kills her with a sharp knife. She is so crazy in her love for Amrita that she undergoes surgery to remove her breasts for she believes that act of hers would make Amrita like her:

> It was a horrible sight. Minx led her to the bed and said, "Sit down. I'll tell you. And then she explained to her slowly and patiently. "It's a tit job. Where do you think I'd gone for a fortnight? Why do you think I wasn't in touch, wasn't around? Well . . . most women go to this plastic surgeon for cosmetic surgery to enhance their breasts—boy! I could give you a few names—but I actually asked him to reduce mine. You know, slice them off. Don't ask me why, but I get the feeling you didn't like them—that their huge size put you off."
>
> Amrita had stared at the sight of Minx with her shirt off and those uneven red scars on her chest . . . for the first time, a feeling of sympathy for the wretched woman before her. She heard Minx's voice cracking as she carried on, "And then I met you. Fell in love. A love so intense I felt my body would burst. I thought I saw revulsion in your eyes when you looked at me, especially when I saw you staring at my ugly enormous breasts. Two weeks ago I decided to chop them off." (627)

After this confession by Minx, Amrita feels pity for Minx and is drawn close to her. Amrita is infatuated with her new relationship with Minx for she feels totally comfortable in it. In fact it has become a pattern of her life. As she later admits to Minx's father: "I began to enjoy it. To respond I became dependent I thought we'd spend our life together." (699)

Their relationship had become so deep that Amrita felt her world is complete with Minx protecting her like a protective lover and providing her with a comfortable home to live in and enough financial security. The only thing that was lacking was that her womb could never be filled as Minx cannot impregnate her with a child as they belong to the same sex. Later, when she marries Rakesh and Minx starts following her, unwilling to let her go, Amrita feels both love and pity for Minx. She cries for help when Minx is caught in fire. She is deeply sorry and yet she does not want to return to that crazy relationship after tasting the happy conjugal relationship with her husband.

In the case of Minx, lesbianism results from her deep hatred of men and fear of deception. Her becoming a lesbian is a form of revolt against the male-dominated society. She wants to show that she is also capable of doing all those things which a man does in the society. Likewise, in *Starry Nights*, the lesbian relationship between Linda and Aasha Rani is a revolt against the patriarchal traditional set up of our society, which allows the sexual relationship of only the heterosexual kind. In man-woman relationship, it is usually the man who has an upper hand. Most women have no guts to voice or react to their partners' feeling of fulfillment in sexual pleasure. In De's novels the picture of male domination in all fields of life is given a vibrant jolt. Woman denounces man as unimportant even on the sexual front as is seen in *Starry Nights* and *Strange Obsession*.

To sum up it may be said that lesbianism is a natural consequence of aspiring for greater independence in a woman's psyche. It is the result of her inner urge to get sexual satisfaction which has been unjustifiably denied to her by her male partner who by and large cares only for his own pleasure and is inconsiderate to her feelings and desires.

As the reputed French woman novelist and critic Simone De Beauvoir observes: "Between women love is contemplative; caresses are intended less to gain possession of the other than gradually to create the self through her; separateness is abolished, there is no struggle, no victory, no defeat; in exact reciprocity each is at once subject and object, sovereign and slave; duality becomes mutuality." Says Colette in *Les Plaisirs*: "The lover takes delight in being sure of caressing the secrets of which she knows, and whose preferences her own body indicates to her." And Renee Vivien's poem (from Sortileges) expresses the same idea: "Our bodies are made alike. . . . Our destiny the same. . . . In you I love my child, my darling, and my sister."[24]

What the new woman's aspirations hint at is that tender approach is an important thing in man-woman relationship and particularly in man's behaviour towards woman. A woman can work up another woman better than a man. The man has to "perform" and after doing it he does not have to be indifferent to his female partner or show lack of care for her. In a recent survey a woman gives the following reasons for her lesbian preference; it is much easier to give in conditionally to a woman, to surrender ego; her skin is soft and smooth, no worry whether my body is "adequate"; no worry about the partner's sexual moral judgement, where I was going to be placed on the spectrum of female frailties (angel or whore). Here surrendering of ego is important, the implication being it is easier to surrender before one's own sex than to the male who already rules, exploits and dominates the female. And herein comes another facet of lesbian behaviour—that is, realizing independence from the male which is another important principle of feminism or Women's Lib Movement. It also has political implications. Hite writes that lesbianism can be political. Sex with another woman could be better "because of the more equal relationship possible. Sex with woman can be a reaction against man and our second class status with them in society."[25] One of the subjects in the Hite survey says, "Sex with a man is often the beginning of a political education. Sex with a woman means independence from man."[26]

Hence the presence of lesbianism in De's novels is a part of the new rebellious woman who wants an equal footing with man. What Linda and Aasha Rani, Minx and Amrita share are manifestations of the new woman who seeks fulfillment of every wish including the wish for sexual fulfillment within her own sex. It is the new woman's drive for self-determination which prompts her to explore new fields like lesbianism. De's depiction of explicit sex between women is a truthful picture of the new reality which is coming up fast in the modern world and its increasingly independent women-folk who are throwing challenges to men in almost all spheres of human activity. Lesbianism, though a resentful term to discuss about in our still conservative Indian society, needs to be understood and deserves to be analyzed even in greater detail. What De has brought out in her novels is an admirably realistic account of the woman's lib today which is a valuable eye-opener to the minds which tend to shut off so many serious realities in the name of obscenity and taboo. If these realities are given due cognizance in a liberal and constructive way, a lot of human reform is possible. De indeed has left no facts untouched in her presentation of the image of the new woman.

Another De novel, *Sultry Days*, takes us into the world of power, sex and guns, the shady side of Mumbai upper class society. Deb the male protagonist attracts popular attention by writing against everyone including Marxists, bureaucrats, businessmen, politicians, artists, writers and so on. This is the only novel of De where the main protagonist is a male. Like all other men of the high society, Deb uses women and throws them out after he has satisfied his physical urge. His popularity goes to his head and he becomes involved with Yashwantbhai, an underworld don, who controls the purse strings of his party and demands huge donations from industrialists and businessmen. Deb is shot after he falls out with Yashwantbhai because he knows too much of the latter's activities.

De presents a group of modern vain upper class women with all their faults. Karen is a rich housewife who takes pride in her exotic good looks. She uses her house like a show room and is always ready to sell off her antiques and furniture to her guests who happen to praise them. Shona, the model from London, knows about all the beautiful women characters and actresses 'from Cleopatra to Sridevi.'[27] To look different and no less attractive she wears a skillfully cut wig to hide a major flaw in her beauty. But, ironically, as the novel observes, her forehead is as large as 'papad.' (782) Another interesting woman is Feroze who wants to be the first Parsee director of Hindi films. She has "lived, breathed and dreamed movies." (814) Kiki is a popular film actress and the ideal woman of Feroze. Kiki's chief rival is Zainab who takes pride in being "the film industry's first unwed mother." (817) The father of their legitimate child is a foreigner who is not connected with the showbiz. It is only the female protagonist Nisha, God's lover, who is shown as a woman who disapproves of the society of these high-class women, a class to which she herself belongs. Through these women characters De sheds significant light on the important issues which give morals of these women a new face.

At this point it would be worthwhile to note that Shobha De takes keen interest in presenting all the facets of the new woman's aesthetic preoccupations. She observes in great detail the interest of her protagonists to enhance their facial beauty and body figure in ways with which high society women outside the novel are quite familiar. An example of their pre-occupations may be quoted here. About maintaining the body figure Anjali in *Socialite Evenings* says:

> Just before I got into the car, I saw a quick flash of the old Anjali. She picked up a strand of my hair. 'Split,' she said tch-tching. 'Do you know your hair is splitting? You must take care of your appearance. I saw your feet also. You haven't been going for pedicures obviously. And am I imagining it or have your gained around the waist? This is the time a woman has to watch it—you let yourself go—and you're finished. I have this wonderful bai who comes and gives me a daily massage. Warm almond oil—divine, divine, divine. I could send her to you once a week. You might have to pay her something extra for coming that distance. But she's worth it. What about workouts? Are you working out regularly? That waist, darling, I don't like what I see there middle-age spread. Most Indian women have a low mentality. Get married and get fat. Disgusting. Anyway, you're lucky to have a good skin. Have you started weekly facials? In case you're looking for someone—this woman who comes home—remember that Parsee female, Farida?—She is now into natural stuff. Apricots, seaweed, cactus—takes care of the lives.' (105)

Or again, when Aasha Rani meets Kishenbhai's film producer for acceptance of her role in films her traditional style make-up is not quite upto his expectations. He is highly sarcastic about her aesthetic sense:

> Why had amma done this to her? Why couldn't she have worn a skirt and blouse or a salwar-kameez? And the make-up-aiiyo, it was terrible. The maroon lipstick, the glittering bindi, the eye-liner that made her eyes look like Ravana's, the tons of blush-on like an angry rash and of course, the layers of light coloured foundation to make her look fair. (246)

When Shobha De is keen to focus attention on the new woman's choice of jewellery she does lot of mind-searching as to what would suit the occasion. Reema in *Snapshots* shows her selection:

> Reema had finalized her jewellery last night. She'd wondered whether her pearls would do the trick—the pink ones from Hongkong. Then she decided to stick to jadav—the simple set her

> mother had presented her. Somehow it gave her confidence. Pearls were so commonplace these days. . . . 'What about your solitaires, Mummy. They go with everything.' Of course, Silly she had it thought of them herself . . . Reema debated over the sari. After all it was her lunch, and she was the host—she was permitted to be overdressed. No. No sari.

She underlines Reema's make-up for the kitty luncheon party:

> Make-up was never a problem for Reema—she was an expert. She'd gone to a grooming class two years ago—the fancy one conducted by an ex-model. She'd picked up all the tricks—how to apply lipstick so her lips looked thinner, how to wear kajal so her eyes seemed larger, how to paint on eyebrows a la filmstar Rekha defining each individual hair so that they appeared longer, how to shade her checks with blusher so they acquired contours—oh how she enjoyed cheating with her bag of tricks?[28]

De's *Snapshots* unveils "the life of six girls of Santa Maria High School, leading predictable mundane lives of domesticity and imagined bliss." (919) They had drifted to their respective worlds of routine marriage and divorce. Swati, one of the most daring of the girls now residing in London, had been asked to write a bold and meaty serial on urban woman. She plans a meeting with her school time friends Reema, Aparna, Surekha, Rashmi and Noor. Though they dislike Swati all of them decide to join the party because right from their school days Swati always had a kind of power over others. Swati is the most powerful among them. She demonstrates her control over men. But all these women are bold and daring. Rashmi comments that mediocre women use "sex as bait or food. It was the shrewd ones who used their brains. And schemed throughout their lives to hold their men, keep them enslaved." (907) Outspoken Swati claims, "We rejoice in our sexuality . . . we do not suppress it, we don't dismiss it. . . . Sex does not threaten us." (977) This psychology definitely lowers the degree of man's power over women.

These modern urban women have transformed themselves from commodities into individuals. Rashmi is an unwed mother; Swati and Aparna are divorcees who are self-assertive enough to reject the sexuality of men. Reema uses her husband to provide herself with material comfort. Marriage seems to have lost its sanctity and significance for her. Reema enjoys illicit relationship with her brother-in-law; Noor's mother is man-crazy; Surekha finds herself more comfortable in her relationship with women than men. Swati considers man to be a commodity that she can acquire in the market. The value system and morality undergo a radical change with these ladies; consequently the hierarchy of males is threatened and it is no longer in a position to exercise its power over the female world. This is the new morality which constantly emerges and becomes visible in Shobha De's image of the new woman.

In *Second Thoughts*, De comes up with the story of Maya, a young and attractive woman who goes into an arranged marriage with Ranjan, a bank executive. She had liked Ranjan at her very first meeting with him. Another reason for liking him was her desire to be a part of the Mumbai world which to her is like a dreamland of glamour and beauty. She hails from an educated middle class family of Calcutta and had dreamed of having a career in designing. But Ranjan turns out to be a Mama's boy who hardly cares for Maya's sentiments. Maya has all the material comforts but she lacks the basic comfort of receiving her husband's love. She is mortified by Ranjan's mother obsession. He wants Maya to follow his mother as her ideal.

Maya suffers an unfulfilled sexual relationship with Ranjan. He turns out to be a cold sexual partner to Maya. She needs physical fulfillment above everything else. She turns to her neighbour's son, Nikhil, who is a college-going boy and much younger to her in years. Maya indulges in a strange relationship with Nikhil whose flirtations give Maya the necessary kick of companionship. Maya has her sexual gratification in one encounter with Nikhil which leaves her satisfied and rejuvenated beyond measure. Maya's ability to rejuvenated beyond measure. Maya's ability to satisfy her urges in these meetings with Nikhil places her among those women of Shobha De who are able to break free from the shackles of social morality even if the experience of freedom is of a short duration.

All the women characters in De's novels are drawn after the life-style of the rich, independent, upper class women. They have left their traditional image far behind. A new set of moral values has been framed by these women as they revel in their glittering aristocratic world. There is no limit to their fantasies and deeds. Their morals may be questionable in the eyes of women or people belonging to the lower strata of society but among their own circle everything they do is the most normal form of womanly behaviour. They brook no interference of any kind in their personal lives. Each one of them seems to have a similar set of morality. In fact De's aesthetic lies in her ability to convey to her readers the sentiments, mentality and life-style of this new class of women which attracts the middle class. De gives a vivid description of these women and their inner world. However reckless this world of women may appear to be, there is a clear message that the new woman is a strong individual who is out to create a new identity for herself in the society. Her promiscuous sexual behaviour may bring her the bad name of being a woman of loose morals. But going by the fact that her male counterparts are indulging in the same, it will be wrong to call them characterless. Whatever they do is a reaction to their immediate surroundings. It is in fact the modern system of education which awakens them to claim equal rights with man.

De's novels appeal so much to the middle class readership for it is the middle class women who are always eager to read and know about the lifestyle of the upper class women. It is they who dream of making it big by joining this highest rung of society which seems so bright and wonderful. Whether the novels make a positive or negative impact on the reader does not count so much. What matters is that they are widely read for all kinds of new experiences, aesthetic sense and morality which are given an altogether new definition. Morality no longer implies demarcation of accepted sexual boundaries but emphasizes values which are derived from the actions of people in the changing social atmosphere. Morality thus becomes a term with changeable meaning which can be redefined from time to time. Shobha De's novels thus call for a redefining of the traditional set of moral values in the light of actions of the fast growing breed of new ultra modern group of ambitious women.

NOTES

1. A.S. Hornby, *Oxford Advanced Learner's Dictionary* (Sixth Edition, 2000), p. 20.
2. Ajay Singh, "The Trouble with Men," *Asiaweek*, Bombay, p. 1.
3. *Ibid.*
4. R.S. Pathak, "Feminist Concerns in Shobha De's Work: A Study in Attitudes," *The Fiction of Shobha De*, ed. Jaydipsinh Dodiya (New Delhi: Prestige, 2000), p. 36.
5. A.S. Hornby, p. 825.
6. Shyam Asnani, "New Morality in the Modern Indo-English Novel: A Study of Mulk Raj Anand, Anita Desai and Nayantara Sahgal," *Indian Women Novelists*, ed. R.K. Dhawan, Vol. I (New Delhi: Prestige, 1991), p. 104.
7. *Ibid.*, p. 105
8. *Ibid.*, p. 113
9. *Ibid.*, p 112
10. *Ibid.*, p. 114
11. *Ibid.*, p. 111.
12. Shobha De, *Socialite Evenings*, in *Shobha De Omnibus* (New Delhi, 1995), p. 128.
13. Shobha De, *Starry Nights*, in *Shobha De Omnibus*, p. 241.
14. Ajay Singh, p. 1.
15. Shobha De, *Sisters*, in *Shobha De Omnibus*, p. 458.
16. Shobha De, *Strange Obsession*, in *Shobha De Omnibus*, p. 628

17. Prabhat Kumar Pandeya, "Tender, Beautiful and Erotic: Lesbianism in *Starry Nights*," *The Fiction of Shobha De*, ed. Jaydipsinh Dodiya, p. 200.
18. *Ibid.*, p. 208.
19. *Loc. cit.*
20. *Ibid.*, p. 205.
21. *Loc. cit.*
22. *Ibid.*, pp. 205-6.
23. Neelam Tikkha, "Lesbian Relationship in *Strange Obsession*," *The Fiction of Shobha De*, ed. Jaydipsinh Dodiya, p. 220.
24. Simone De Beauvoir, *The Second Sex* (London: The New English Library, 1966), p. 155.
25. Prabhat Kumar Pandeya, "Tender, Beautiful and Erotic," p. 206.
26. *Loc. cit.*
27. Shobha De, *Sultry Days*, in *Shobha De Omnibus*, p. 782.
28. Shobha De, *Snapshots*, in *Shobha De Omnibus*, p. 918.

Realism: Lifelike Characters

The word realism implies "a way of seeing, accepting and perceiving situations as they really are without any colouring of our emotion or false hopes."[1] It shows things as they are in reality. In Shobha De's novels this kind of realism is given full play. Her novels present lifelike situations of individuals belonging to the rich and powerful upper class of modern Mumbai, a prominent Asiatic metropolis which is culturally at par with its Western counterparts like London or New York. Shobha De belongs to this glossy circle of the ultra rich metropolitan society and is able to project an intimate picture of this society exposing many pleasant as well as unpleasant details about the lifestyles of some of its representative members. People who belong to this set-up are rich, powerful and famous. They lead wild and reckless lives. They are usually top bureaucrats, business magnates, film producers and directors and the stinking rich members of this glamorous high society.

The portrayal of women of this fast world is fascinating and it is these women who are the subject of this study. Women belonging to this society are independent, ruthlessly ambitious and highly self-assertive. Women belonging to this class demand equal rights with men. They are hell-bent to demolish every existing rule and question any norm which subordinates women to men or accords them a place subservient to men.

The Indian upper class society and its women are fully laid bare in De's novels. However the high level of freedom enjoyed by these women has both positive as well as negative sides. De exposes the amazing and the fascinating as well as the abhorrent aspects of this society Women of this society are an enigma and it is this quality which makes them a subject that provokes serious study.

In her first novel, *Socialite Evenings*, the protagonist becomes an eager aspirant of the Mumbai high society soon after her middle class bureaucrat father gets posted in the glittering city. Becoming wildly ambitious Karuna defies her father's strict conservative rules and jumps into the glamour world of modelling. Thc modelling career introduces her to the Mumbai's high society. Her meeting with Anjali, wife of the rich playboy Abbas Tyabji (Abe), is crucial and instrumental to her development and progress in becoming the new woman. Anjali virtually becomes Karuna's mentor.

The eagerness of an educated middle class ambitious woman to be a part of the high society is clearly seen in Karuna. She is proud of being acquainted with Anjali. Anjali's display of her riches fascinates Karuna beyond measure: "Her fragrance washed over me, . . . Then there it was, an enormous, finned Impala in silver grey. It glided up like a gigantic swan negotiating its way past handcart pullers, pedestrians, taxis and local buses. It was the perfect vehicle for her."[2]

Karuna enjoys belonging to the high society at Anjali's initiation. She grows so self-conscious that in course of time she becomes almost a rival to Anjali. Anjali accuses Karuna of her insatiable appetite for sex. This happens when Karuna starts dating the New Delhi based filmmaker in London. Karuna marries but her marriage turns out to be a cold, loveless affair. Her husband is not at all bothered about her sentiments and desires. He is busy with his own rise in the corporate world. Karuna had married him only with an eye on his social status and money. She confesses that she had married "the wrong man for the wrong reasons at the wrong time. He is just an average Indian husband—unexciting, uninspiring, untutored."[2] Karuna learns from Ritu, whom she chances upon at a finance director's party that "men like dogs could be conditioned through reward and punishment." (44) Locked up in a fragile and futile marriage Karuna's life is one of emotional frigidity. There is no communication between the partners. Karuna enters into an extra-marital relationship with her husband's friend, Krish.

Anjali and Karuna are now companions in evil. Both of them are involved in licentious relationships. Anjali has several involvements with her male friends. She makes wild sexual adventures, first with the Belgian photographer who has come to photograph Karuna's modelling postures, then with the young boy Karan who is approximately her daughter's age. After her divorce from Abe, she once again looks for a new companion who can fill her husband's place and whose riches could be used by her to keep up with her luxurious lifestyle. Anjali gets her desired mate once again in the filthy rich Kumar Bhandhari who is a gay and who has his own crazy style of passionate sessions with young boys. The sex maniac Anjali ultimately becomes a totally sexless woman. She leaves Kumar alone with his own fantasies and in return gets the financial security and enjoys luxuries without which she cannot live. The crazy nymphomaniac turns suddenly into a religious-minded devotee.

She may have changed her attitude towards life but her previous wild deeds take their toll on her young daughter Mimi who becomes a drug addict. Anjali fails in her role as a mother. Obsessed with her own happiness and comfort, she completely neglects her daughter.

Karuna and Anjali are not the only women who succumb to immoral love-adventures. Another woman who behaves similarly is Ritu. Ritu's marriage goes haywire because she indulges in promiscuous relationships. Despite the fact that she is married she falls for Gul, an underworld Don and a smuggler who has enormous wealth. Her love relationship turns her into a mere pimp whose duty is to procure women for Gul and his friends. In utter frustration she starts drinking heavily, consumes drugs and puts on a lot of weight. After all her crazy loitering in the world of unfaithful lovers she returns to her husband who takes her back and forgives her. The wild adventures of these modern society women clearly reflect the tendency in the new women exposed to affluence and extra-marital relationships and their impact on their family life and children. It is a clear warning to both the wife and the husband to bear in mind the possible influence of their wild aspirations on their children and the society.

At the end of three years of torrid romance between Karuna and Krish the latter shows his reluctance to tie the wedding knot with the former. Karuna realizes that their affair was a mere sex game. Divorced by her husband on the one hand, she breaks off with Krish on the other and finally gets liberated from both husband and lover and becomes independent. Yet despite getting the space she craved for she is terribly upset over the termination of her unwanted pregnancy by undergoing hysterectomy and is angry at her husband's taking to another woman. She is compelled to take up odd jobs at first but later with Anjali's help she finds a lucrative job which helps her to support her crazy lifestyle. Once money starts flowing in, Karuna finds herself free and able to look at life afresh. Freed of her marital obligations she takes care of her old parents and it gives her satisfaction to be of some use to them. She finally finds freedom. She declines her husband's proposal to come back to him. She finds repulsive the idea of losing this new-found happiness of being single and becoming master of her own self. Even though Girish Shridhar, the famous art film maker, approaches her with a marriage proposal she is in no mood to accept it instantaneously:

> I feel all closed up and insulated. I need little time. I am discovering myself. I enjoyed this little patch of independence. I'm reconnecting with my parents—they need me. I am enjoying their presence. . . . Don't rush me please. (60)

She apprehends that even if Girish and herself had lot of common interest between them she could not be happy with any man. Her present state of independence gave her so much of contentment that she cannot think of marrying again and binding herself to anyone.

Pleading from the opposite angle, Karuna's mother informs her of the problems faced by women in a patriarchal society. Yet she also speaks of the various kinds of real difficulties and hardships a woman living single and alone had to encounter: "A woman cannot live alone. It is not safe. We are here today but who knows about tomorrow. A woman needs a man's protection. Society can be very cruel." (186)

De is quite realistic in making the protagonist perceive the stark reality of the practical difficulties of women living alone. Karuna also knows how Anjali had been terrified by the thought of remaining single. Her mention of an experience of a man trying to take advantage of her because she did not have her own man to stand by her is a commonplace experience of women in every society. She is sensible enough and well aware of her difficulties of remaining single in this society. Yet she is firm on her stand that she would not share her life with any man, no matter how difficult the situation she may be faced with. She does not want to jeopardize her future by bringing a wrong person into her life, spoiling the peace of the home which she had built with her hard-earned money. She is different from Anjali who out of fear to be single marries a man who turns out to be a homo.

Towards the end of the novel, Karuna meets Ranbir Roy, a reporter in *The Washington Times*. She strikes up a relationship with him but declines his invitation to accompany him to Washington as an assistant. When Karuna confidently says in the end "Single is good for me," Ranbir comments: "You are now disgustingly self-assured and revoltingly self sufficient." (200)

The image of the new woman now emerges much clearer than before. This woman belongs to the class of the independent women who have no consideration for the social bindings and who consider marriage just a relationship for one's convenience. She is determined to make it clear that she does not want to be confined to one particular place, the home, like the traditional Indian women nor is she even like those modern women who are educated, have ideas of independence but could go no farther than merely contemplating their new ideas. Karuna's character is a trendsetter for the rest of the women who want to live life the new way. De presents realistic, factual details about the middle class women who aspire to belong to high society and acquire a new life for themselves. Throughout the novel De directly and satirically attacks the men of the Indian society for their derogatory attitude toward and the uncivil treatment of their women folk.

After *Socialite Evenings*, De's second novel *Starry Nights* again created a stir in the feminist literature of conservative India. It traces the career graph of Aasha Rani who rises as a famous heroine in the dark and sinister world of Mumbai film world. She emerges as an unrivalled actress of great beauty with an insatiable sexual urge. She indulges in indiscriminate promiscuous affairs with the notables of the film industry—producers, actors, directors, cameramen, business tycoons and people from non-film world—and finally enters into a lesbian relationship.

The chief propeller of Aasha Rani's first tryst with sexual adventure is her mother who is eager to make money, pushes her daughter into the film world to become a star. She takes her daughter to well-known sex-hungry directors and producers. She directs her fifteen-year daughter to work in blue films. Fascinated by the sensuality of Aasha Rani's forty-inch bust, the hungry wolves of Bollywood happily give her a big professional lift.

Aasha Rani's own strong sexual drive may be the result of her anger to avenge her father's ill-treatment of her mother. Perhaps what adds to her anger is the nightmarish experience of her own uncle exploiting her sexually. Her father, a renowned film producer in Madras, led a reckless life with other women leaving her mother and their three kids to starve and fend for themselves. She recollects sadly:

> When appa had left, amma had aged overnight. She looked worn-out middle aged though she must be in her late twenties. Aasha Rani remembered a succession of dubious 'mamas' turning up at their place and taking amma out on mysterious missions. She'd come back late in the night, smelling strange and looking sleepy.[3]

This is a very realistic presentation of a commonplace experience of how even the closest relations of a person try to exploit and take advantage when one is suffering and in distress.

Shobha De is no doubt a past master in narrating the incidents connected with sexual motifs. But as soon as she takes the situation to be narrated in hand she becomes more and more matter of fact. Her narration of the events appears to be fictional but soon the stark realism of the events overtakes fiction. The spicy narration of Aasha Rani's professional ambition is mixed with an element of obscenity which is highly captivating. Aasha Rani's rise in her career is simultaneously accompanied by her downfall. She finds herself in the hands of Kishenbhai, a small film producer. He is her first sexual exploiter followed later by a host of other hungry men. Throughout her sensual affairs with the big names of the film industry, her mother acts as her pimp. Aasha Rani starts seeing man as nothing but a sexual object. When she rises to the top of her profession she falls in love with the top hero Akshay Arora who is a married man. Aasha Rani has a long and passionate affair with Akshay. She even has terrible fights with Akshay's wife Malini who hates Aasha Rani for disturbing their married life. Aasha Rani also acts like the typical mistress, unabashed even when Malini accuses her of being a sex maniac:

> Malini screamed, "SEX! That is all you have—SEX! That is what women like you use. Cheap bitches, part your legs and let any man in. Sex, sex, sex, dirty filthy sex! Perverts! you must be a pervert." (264)

Aasha Rani's desire for Akshay puts her in humiliating situations. Things become so bad that when she goes uninvited to a film launch party of Akshay she is rebuked and beaten up mercilessly by him. She goes almost mad in her love for Akshay; when he declines to marry her, she cuts her wrist and contemplates suicide. Though she is saved, she is dejected and unhappy. In spite of her fame and wealth she misses one big thing in her life, i.e., true love. A number of men are ready to be in bed with her but not one is honest enough to marry her. Almost all her affairs are with married men and that is one reason of her failure to achieve true love in life. Disappointed in her desire for fulfillment in love, Aasha Rani finds herself indulging in a lesbian relationship with Linda, a film magazine journalist. De is quite explicit in presenting details of their amorous relationship:

> There was no resistance left any more, Aasha Rani's entire body was floating—her mind was adrift. She let her arms drop to her sides as Linda's warm thigh wedged itself between her and her hand moved between Aasha Rani's legs. 'Close your eyes, let me do to you what no man could have done. . . . My hands, my mouth, my tongue, my thighs will set your body on fire. . . . Enjoy it . . . enjoy it . . . Oh . . . I've been dying for you all these months. And now you are mine at last.' (288)

Not only in the presentation of factual details of Aasha Rani's rise in her professional career but also in the competitive spirit involved in these promotions De makes things as clear as possible.

The new woman in Linda is concerned to promote her career interest. Even though she shares physical intimacy with

Aasha Rani, Linda does not hesitate to write against Aasha Rani when she comes back from New Zealand. Like all other characters in the novel, she is also guided by professional self-interest and would not like human relationships to come in the way of achieving those interests.

When she is at the peak of her career Aasha Rani marries a foreigner, Jamie (Jay) Phillips, whom she had met in Wellington. She is grateful to Jay for loving her honestly. She knew no man of high status in Indian society who would be willing to marry an actress. She gives birth to a daughter Sasha and lives a life of quiet domesticity with Jay's loving arms always ready to receive her. Finally, she fulfils her long-cherished wish to have a family.

On Jay's strong persuasion that she needed to go back to India Aasha Rani returns to her home country. Moreover, her mother too makes a strong suggestion that she would need to stay in India in case she wanted to resume her acting in films. The stay was necessary to push up her acting fees.

Aasha Rani finds her sister Sudha Rani already established as a successful film actress. Between the two sisters there develops some professional rivalry, though the rivalry is felt only by her sister Sudha. Aasha Rani is shocked at her sister's hostile attitude towards her. Another problem emerges as her father lies ailing and needs her support. But she is reluctant to look after him for she wants to go back to New Zealand with Jay.

However, Aasha Rani stays back and joins films once again. She is offered not the lead role but the role of a mother in which she is not interested. Professional unhappiness is followed by personal unhappiness. While Akshay's death comes as a rude shock to her, her daughter phones her, crying that she misses her and that her father spends most of his time with Nanny. Aasha Rani goes back to New Zealand. There she is shocked to find that her daughter finds herself closer to Nanny than herself. Jay openly admits his love for Nanny. After this sad incident Aasha Rani goes to London to hide herself. She finds herself lonely and totally broken down.

The novel ends with Aasha Rani imagining her daughter's return to India to become a popular heroine. Despite all the lust, exploitation and deceptions she had faced as a film actress, she still dreams of her daughter joining films and making a name as a famous actress: "Aasha Rani suddenly imagines her daughter's fresh, innocent face gracing movie hoardings and gossip magazines. Sasha had the makings of a star. The Golden girl of the silver screen!" (405)

The novel projects the reality of Mumbai film world. The film world is full of nasty, lustful and shady characters. Yet it is not an easy task for the new entrant to get a place in this world. The novel depicts the struggle of a young woman to make it to this colourful world with all its difficulties and shame. The price Aasha Rani has to pay to become the number one heroine is awe-inspiring. De's closeness and familiarity with the film world as a journalist might have somewhat facilitated her to portray it in fine detail even though the veracity of the details given may be a matter of her personal observation and opinion.

In De's third novel, *Sisters*, the theme of the new woman attempting to assert herself in this not too-friendly world is evident. The story begins in the highly corrupt world of big business and the two lusty half-sisters—Mallika and Alisha—who are in keen competition to outdo each other.

Consequent upon the death of her parents in an air crash Mallika or Mikki Malhotra finds herself handling her father's industries which are on the brink of collapse. Mikki finds the situation challenging. She renounces all her girlish dreams of going back to America, and takes up the tough job of controlling and running her sprawling industries. Good sense dawns on her as she realizes that instead of running them alone she had better invite her sister Alisha to join her and handle the business together. Earlier, Alisha was hostile to Mikki because she had received huge wealth from her father which was more than enough for her to lead a luxurious life. But Mikki has full faith in human values and she realizes that whenever Alisha was by her side she felt a lot of comfort and solace despite Alisha's indifference.

Mikki faces hard times as the industries were going nearly bankrupt but she was determined to save them. Shanay her cousin advises her to borrow money from her rich fiancé Navin. But Navin fails her for he is so dependent on his mother for this action. Irked by his attitude Mikki calls off her engagement with him. In her anxiety she meets Binny Malhotra, a big business tycoon who had won her heart. Binny woos her with extravagant luxury and attention. Mikki knows Binny too was no simple man but a shark of a man, but she cannot avoid overlooking his real character due to the exigency of having to save her failing business. Her friend Amy cannot but advise her to marry Binny: "The quickest way to shoot to the top is to tie up with Malhotra. And I'm being very practical when I tell you this—what's the worst thing that could happen in that alliance? A disastrous marriage can always be put behind you darling . . . divorce isn't what it used to be." (468)

Marriage becomes for the new woman a means of manipulating business interests, not of promoting welfare of the family. Mikki marries Binny but, as it turns out, for all the wrong reasons. Contrary to her expectations, Binny turns out to be a big womanizer. He had already got a mistress Urmi and her two children. Mikki is shattered and confounded. Though she is legally married to Binny, the latter's mind is with Urmi and their children. Although Mikki finds it hard to digest the fact that she has been cheated by Binny, yet she loves the man to madness. All her property has been transferred to Binny after their marriage in the hope that it would facilitate better business transactions. But nothing of that kind happens. Instead her marriage and life becomes miserable.

Binny no longer allows her to go to office. He even commands her to stay at home.

Mikki turns into a submissive wife. Binny cannot allow her to work in an office because of his family tradition which does not permit women to work outside the home. Mikki is willing for such a compromise if only he would notice her, listen to her and give due regard to her individuality. But nothing of that sort happens. Instead the worst happens as Binny divorces her. She finally realizes that there is no future for her in playing the weak female and always looking for man's support. She turns to her not-so-sympathetic sister Alisha for emotional support. Alisha, unlike Mikki, feels insecure and leads a wild life. She hates Mikki for capturing all their father's love while she herself was neglected. She is so jealous of her that she imitates Mikki in almost everything. She feels happy whenever Mikki is in trouble. She even mixes with Mikki's former boy friend Navin, as it gives her immense pleasure to acquire whatever belongs to Mikki. Alisha gets involved with Dr. Kurien knowing full well that he was a married man with children. She becomes so crazy in her relationship with this man that she becomes a drug addict. Mikki comes to rescue Alisha when the latter goes through difficult times after the death of her mother. She helps Alisha to overcome the difficult days of her life.

Both women finally reconcile with each other and decide to face the world together as friends and sisters. They had experienced enough dejection and cheating and suffering in their youth as to have learnt the futility of seeking friendship with men. They see a new happiness in each other's company. They resolve to face the world together as strong and capable women who want to determine their own future with or without the help of men.

What De has crafted in this novel is again the new women with ambitious ideas and a strong motivation to define the world in their own terms. Rich, intelligent and smart, these women prove themselves as being not inferior to men but superior to and even better than men.

Strange Obsession is yet another path-breaking work of Shobha De. This novel treats a very unusual and sensational topic i.e., lesbianism. It is a topic which is still taboo and not easy to discuss. It is a subject of great curiosity and debate in every society. The novel revolves around two young women Amrita, an upcoming model and Minx a lesbian. Amrita comes from a noble and educated middle class family, who lands in Mumbai in search of a career in modelling. She meets Minx, the high flying daughter of the Inspector General of Police. She takes a fancy for Amrita and that begins a horrifying saga of sex, lies and violence. Minx feels a strange attraction toward Amrita the moment she sees her. Amrita too finds a new understanding of her at their very first encounter which, in fact, affects Amrita deeply: "She was used to receiving compliments. She had been receiving them all her life. But let alone a woman no man had even looked on her the way Minx just had."[4]

Minx accompanies Amrita everywhere and does not leave her alone. She follows and guards her wherever she goes like a possessive lover. Amrita does not feel happy at Minx's strange behaviour towards her but ultimately with long coaxing succumbs to the temptation of her sexual entrapment by Minx. This is because Minx provides Amrita with all the comforts of life—a nice house, sex and money. But Amrita is aware that this could not carry on for long. After all Minx could never be a substitute for a real man.

Minx in her wild craze for Amrita murders her rival model Lola. Minx is so infatuated with Amrita that she is ready to do anything for her. As she says: "What more do I have to do to prove myself? Kill? I will do that too. Just tell me . . . who? You want me to kill someone? Anyone. I'll do it." (607)

Minx's obsession with Amrita is almost hysterical. She desires every competitor in Amrita's modelling career to be removed from her way. She had attacked Lola with acid. She is now so crazy in her love of Amrita that she would like to suppress and wipe out any sign of femininity in her body. She undergoes surgery to remove her own breast. Amrita is struck with horror when Minx shows her bare chest with uneven red scars left behind by the surgery. Amrita is moved and sad to see Minx's situation and develops great sympathy for her. Amrita is finally drawn to her:

> Minx removed her clothes one by one and placed them neatly on a chair close to the bed. Amrita was suddenly conscious, very conscious of Minx's touch as each nerve ending of her body came alive under her probing fingers and tongue. . . . After what must have been two hours, they finally fell into a light sleep with Amrita's head cradled in the crook of Minx's arm, their legs entangled. (628)

Amrita falls for Minx's love. Whether it is natural or unnatural it does not matter to her any more. It is only after Rakesh comes into her life that Amrita withdraws from her relationship with Minx. Minx looks for Rakesh's blood for she blames Rakesh for making Amrita ditch her love. Minx is wild, almost mad as she gives enough pain to Amrita and Rakesh when at the point of a gun she makes them make love in front of her. Minx humiliates both Rakesh and Amrita. Amrita is sorry for Minx when her oppressor dies silently with multiple burns.

The new perception of life for the new women is unrestrained and full of options: they have no hassles in choosing even women as their sex partners. This is evident not only in *Strange Obsession* but also in *Starry Nights* where Linda and Aasha Rani show a similar relationship. Liberal ideas sweep across their minds so much that whatever fulfillments they demand they get. However it does not necessarily mean that their financial status, emotional and physical happiness and security may be possible only in the company of men. These new women display a different attitude towards everything with the result that the new world they create at first looks so unreal and fantastic. Yet that is the reality that ultimately prevails within the world of the new women of De's novels.

In *Sultry Days*, De takes on a completely new approach towards dealing with the women's world. In this novel also the women are crazy for men; they challenge men and beat them at their own game. But here the women are shown to be not just blind hitters; they are committed and want equal response from men. Nisha the protagonist loves Deb despite his shabby appearance and dirty habits. He has matted locks of hair unwashed for a couple of days, smokes 'beedies' (local cigarettes made from leaves) and is a man of loose morals. His attitude towards girls is scandalous; he uses them and then discards them. Deb despite his dirty looks and habit is a master of many languages—German, French and Spanish. While at school, he had also read Chaucer and Karl Marx.

Shobha De's narratives descend to realistic level when she deals with the frustrated or distressed women. The element of fantasy is replaced by the commonplace realism of daily life. An instance of it is the differences which severed relations between Nisha and God in *Sultry Days*. God and Nisha's relationship turned cold after the former starts caring less and less for his self-respect. Having tasted power and money during his association with an art magazine *Plume*, God's sole interest is to acquire money and power. Contrary to his attitude Nisha wants everything in life to be achieved through sheer labour. She shuns the life of glamour and the fast life into which she can step any time, being a part of this high society. God's new way of life does not interest her. She explains her utter repulsiveness to God's new style of living which had begun sowing the seeds of discord and estrangement between them:

> No I didn't like what was happening to God at all. We were beginning to see less and less of each other now that he didn't need to touch me for cash that often. He was getting ahead professionally, meeting all the VIPs in town, interviewing culture-vulture and generally being wooed by 'all those who mattered' in the high life in the city.[5]

Feeling that God was no longer committed to their relationship and that he had been swept too far away from their usual simple world, Nisha decides to live life in her own way. She blames Yashwantbhai for the unwelcome change in God. Nisha blasts the dark world of Yashwantbhai with whom God had tied up. She starts exposing Yashwantbhai and also his underworld connections in her write-ups. Nisha's bold action is supported by her mother and also by a social activist Pratimaben who unravels and brings to public notice Yashwantbhai's atrocities on his former mistress, Pramila.

Nisha emerges as a strong, determined and fearless woman who is ready to face any danger that may come her way as a result of confrontation with Yashwantbhai. God no longer has a strong hold over her. She is now independent and seeks to have a link with the common men and women especially of the working middle class and work for their welfare sympathizing with the underdog. She sees herself as one belonging to their class. She has a great admiration for the people belonging to this class, as she thought of them on her way to see God in the hospital:

> It hadn't registered at all. I didn't even want to know the detail. Instead I concentrated on the dabawallahs charging of the railway station and hurtling down the streets bearing home cooked lunches for thousands of down-town office goers. All sorts of pictures flashed through my mind; I thought of the wives who wake up at 5 a.m., to start cooking for their husbands so that the lunch could be ready at 8.30—the time the dabawallah arrived at the doorstep to pick up the lunch box. And I wondered what sort of lives these couples had? Did they communicate or merely talk.
>
> I envied these women and their uncomplicated lives. All they had to bother about was getting the daba ready on time for the da-

> bawallah. Nobody of theirs ever got shot. Nobody threatened them through the mail or over the phone. (866)

This is a very commonplace scene from the daily run of Mumbai life where the small working class women are busy keeping lunch boxes (daba) ready to be lifted and carried by trains to various destinations. The woman realizes that there are always evil forces in the world she has to face. She has the necessary strength to resist the nasty painter Iqbal who was at the point of raping her. She blames herself for the folly of having fallen into his company: "A voice within me kept repeating irritatingly. 'You asked for it. Don't say you didn't; you knew when you climbed those stairs with him and entered this place, exactly what was in store for you. Don't blame him. Blame yourself, you little fool.'" (820)

It is a commonplace situation that De describes here. The women have to face such odd situations. The image of the new emancipated woman who faces such situation is also seen throughout the novel, particularly, when Nisha with a tinge of dislike narrates about this new group:

> They carried the awesome weight of an M.B.A. degree (I.I.M. Ahmedabad or any of the better American business schools like Wharton or Harvard) on their padded shoulders. These were no-nonsense women who had 'take me seriously' written all over them. They even wear business suits to work and carried burgundy, coloured briefcases. . . . Even the married ones insisted on being addressed as 'Ms' or stuck to their maiden names. (792)

These women in their hurry to stress their individuality and become rich will go as far as possible to achieve their goal. Like Pramila, the Nagpur woman, her character very much embodies the new woman. She has everything a woman could aspire for—a husband with a well paid job, lovely children and even a two-wheeler for herself to move around. She also has the talent for writing poetry. She left her loving family to make a niche for herself in the high society of Mumbai. Her fame shoots up as soon as her poems are published in English translation. She administers a shock to her husband when she divorces him and leaves the house along with her two daughters to become free from all scruples. Her meeting with Yashwantbhai and becoming his mistress had created further problems. She had become a victim of his lust. Having become pregnant she is threatened by him for trying to force him to accept her and the unborn child. She is forced to go into hiding. Pramila is brought out in the public eye by Pratimaben and Nisha's mother. Pramila with their support exposes Yashwantbhai.

The novel thus revolves around women who are strong and confident. These women know what they want. The-not so-pleasant side of the lives of these women who live unconventional and fast lives is in consonance with the temper of the modern times particularly with the new trends of life of the sophisticated socialite women whose portraits have been drawn by De and other feminist writers. Again in *Snapshots*, De draws a very realistic image of the upper class metropolitan women and their unconventional life-style. The six school friends Swati, Aparna, Reema, Rashmi, Surekha and Noor had drifted apart after finishing school. Swati proposes that they have a get-together since she had come back to India after staying in London for a long time. She has, no doubt, come to India with a purpose, that is, to write a bold serial on urban women. She thought her five friends would be the best means of getting the desired material for such a serial. As such, she never discloses to the other five friends the real idea behind their get-together.

All the women in *Snapshots* lead interesting lives and their characters reflect the image of the new woman in every aspect. Swati is the most striking and powerful among the six women. She is now a resident of London and she shows an unfair attitude towards her five friends as is evident from the way she views them. She has led the life of a whore or a super-bitch like the ones shown in the American soap operas.

While in India, Swati is the most daring of the six friends. She had married and then divorced her husband and now returns to England to remarry there. The concept of marriage among these new breed of women is no longer that of a sacred tie. To them all marriage is just a transaction of convenience and hence meaningful as long as it is useful. Swati marries, divorces and remarries. Again, Rashmi is an unwed mother. Aparna is a divorcee; Reema uses her husband for her material comfort and enjoys a promiscuous relationship with her brother-in-law Randhir. Surekha is married but shares a lesbian relationship with Dolly: "Surekha too couldn't imagine life without Dolly. Their lives had become inextricably intertwined. Dolly and Surekha like a happily married couple. . . . Just enough physical familiarity to promise regular comfort."[6]

Noor is the only one of them who suffers because she is weak-willed and submissive. She is deserted by her boyfriend Amir before she is even fully aware of their love. Her brother Nawaz commits incest with her. Both her boyfriend and her brother had caused deep scars on her young mind. Noor is the only weak traditional woman represented in the novel and her final release from her mental torment comes when she commits suicide at the end of the novel.

All the other five women lead lives on the fast tract. They live their lives to the fullest. For them men are secondary, their own selves are of primary importance. They cannot tolerate any action of men which denigrates their worth or personality. They spurn the idea of being treated like the weak traditional housewives. An example of this is the bickering between Rohit and Aparna:

> She'd taunt him: 'I thought you were the New Man. I expected you to care and share. But you're like any other husband. The same old double standards.' . . . Rohit would smile sadistically, 'Too bad you miscalculated. Sure I have double standards. I bring home the bread. You cook. Easy.' Aparna would retort furiously, 'don't forget I bring home the bread too. I am a serious career person. When we married, you respected my priorities. You knew what you were

getting into. If you'd wanted a housemaid, you should have married one.' (890)

The consequences of such bickering can be anticipated from a real life experience of a couple that fails to compromise. No wonder Aparna walks out of her marriage and takes to another man Prem as her lover. Rashmi the unwed mother sees the sad part of life after she is left high and dry by the wealthy but miserly film-maker Parminder (Pips) with his baby in her womb. However, undaunted by her suffering she gathers enough strength to bring up Pips Junior by herself but in the process she becomes a prostitute: "Little Pips had grown up in the company of a succession of 'uncles'—men hungry for sex—who drifted in and out of his mother's untidy bed. Often, he'd wake up in the middle of the night and drift sleepily in Rashmi's room to find yet another stranger between her sheets." (904)

Instances of similar situation, of women suffering and falling prey to the sex-hunters to overcome their financial or other difficulties, are certainly real-life situations. De has capitalized on such real life situations in order to show how the new women successfully cope with the problems of life created by their male counterparts. The resultant image of the new woman is that of a woman who is bold enough to rise to the occasion and by exploiting all her potentialities becomes self-reliant. The portrait of Swati is a further illustration of the new woman's self-confidence in exploring her potentialities. The London-based Swati never feels any scruples to act in dirty English films as long as she gets her money. She attends parties with rich gentlemen and high officials of the state. She thus manages to become a popular figure in the London high society using her body as the main bait: "Swati made it to the covers of the most major film magazines, and *Vanity Fair*, the number one society monthly, featured her in an eight-page profile which had her lolling languorously against a painted elephant, wrapped in cobras, semi-naked on a bed of nails and making eyes at a tiger." (904)

De's images of the new woman resemble the ones depicted in the day-to-day wall-posters in public streets. Swati reminds one of a news item widely covered by international media and London tabloids concerning an Indian woman Pamela Bordes who had actually made her way up as a top influential woman through her sexual connections with mighty British politicians and other powerful shots of London society.

The basic moral issues of life are in fact given a different dimension by these women. These women are strong, determined and have no hassles in behaving in any manner they like. Swati is perhaps the most appropriate and suitable replica of the new woman delineated by Shobha De in this novel.

The presentation of the new woman is again marked in De's novel *Second Thoughts*. It is the story of a young middle class Bengali girl Maya who goes to Mumbai after an arranged marriage to a foreign returned Bengali boy Ranjan. Maya is eager to catch the life-style of Mumbai but her husband turns out to be a cold Indian male who believes that by marrying the girl he had bestowed a favour upon her.

Disillusioned with her husband, Maya finds herself trapped in an unfeeling marriage. In her depression she enters into a strange relationship with her college-going neighbour, Nikhil, with whom she made enjoyable company in her dull moments. He enlivens her spirit and seems to understand her better than her husband, thus giving Maya a feeling of comfort which she had desperately looked for because her yearning for Ranjan's love could not find the fulfillment she needed. Once Ranjan returns from Calcutta after ten days, Maya shyly snuggles up to him and caresses him but to her shame and horror Ranjan jumps back and scolds her:

> jumping back as though he had received an electric shock. He had lain trembling in bed for a long time, his breathing heavy, his eyes screwed shut.
>
> 'Stop behaving like a cheap woman. A prostitute,' he had muttered before turning around and going to sleep. (259)

A distressed woman is thus liable to seek out comfort from some other source. Her friendship with Nikhil helps her to overcome her despair and the corroding feeling of emptiness in her married life. Their sexual union heals the wounds of Maya's loveless marriage. The act itself is a natural corollary to an inner urge to satisfy her long suppressed desire to discover love and passion for life. Even though Maya leads a very suppressed existence, her marriage finally breaks down all moral codes. She goes out with Nikhil to explore Mumbai in her husband's absence. The extra-sexual act thus proves to be the final blow to the marital bond with Ranjan in her quest for freedom.

Yet, in conformity with the traditional pattern of Indian life, Maya returns to her husband and their monotonous world. But she knows that she had already set her marriage bond on fire by enjoying herself in those few minutes of forbidden pleasure with Nikhil. De thus realistically points to the traditional way of life of a common Indian woman who is taught to conform and preserve and live upto the pious bond of matrimony. *Second Thoughts* is the only De novel which sketches the life of the higher middle class and in the character of Maya presents woman who apparently conforms to the norms of the society but secretly breaks them when she finds them unjust and unacceptable.

Shobha realistically portrays Indian high society in almost all her novels. Herself being a part of that society, she dares to portray the seamy side of both the traditional and the modern ways of living of the new woman. She gives a very clear picture of the new woman who resides in the fast world of this aristocratic circle.

De is out and out a practical realist. She points to the fact that these new women cannot succeed unless they are economically strong. As she once said, "Eventually, everything boils down to money—the great leveller. There can be no talk of independence for woman without economic self-sufficiency. An independent mind or free spirit is meaningless so long as the body and soul are being kept together by somebody else."[8]

De's women work to make themselves economically independent. They are usually well established women with high profile careers. They are not afraid to take up challenges to achieve their desired goals. Marriage is not regarded as essential to their advancement by these women. On the contrary marriages are treated as mere games of catching rich grooms which can be thrown away once they become non-functional or do not yield economic benefits, or become hindrances in achieving their desired goals.

De seems determined to bring into clear view and analyze the lives of those new women. She focuses mainly on their fast lives like the way these women have freely invaded the taboo topic of sex. The sinister sins these women commit and the dark relations they clandestinely carry on are given full blown exposure. De also brings into focus the much covered area of lesbianism in her novels. She endeavours to scan all aspects of the women's lives of the high aristocratic society. Sometimes there is a tinge of bitter malice also towards these people as she narrates the real life-like sagas of the well known attractive figures in her novels.

It can therefore be said that Shobha De's women are realistic to the core. She has successfully drawn the image of the New Woman who resides in the aristocratic world of Indian high society. This image is not of the weak and submissive woman fearing her domination by her husband. This new woman is dynamic, strong and highly confident. She no longer lives at the mercy of the family and society. She in fact represents a newly emerging class of women who are sure of their minds and body, and who can comfortably demand their pound of flesh from their partners and the society on their own terms.

In conclusion, it may be noted that on the one hand De's fictional world arouses curiosity and interest and on the other invites a sympathetic denunciation of the world of the new woman which is not quite sane. The works of this "high priestess of gossip and innuendo" have been regarded as the "equivalent of Hindi films with their peephole voyeurism"[9] Shobha De once said: "I write with a great deal of empathy towards women. Without waving the feminist flag, I feel very strongly about the women situation."[10] It would therefore be appropriate to study in greater detail Shobha De's sympathies with the New Woman, a task that I undertake in the next chapter.

NOTES

1. A.S. Hornby, *Oxford Advanced Learner's Dictionary of Current English* (Sixth Edition, 2000), p. 1055.
2. Shobha De, *Socialite Evenings*, in *Shobha De Omnibus* (New Delhi,1995), p. 4.
3. Shobha De, *Starry Nights*, in *Shobha De Omnibus*, p. 279.
4. Shobha De, *Sisters*, in *Shobha De Omnibus*, p. 468.
5. Shobha De, *Strange Obsession*, in *Shobha De Omnibus*, p. 574.
6. Shobha De, *Sultry Days*, in *Shobha De Omnibus*, p. 778.
7. Shobha De, *Snapshots*, in *Shobha De Omnibus*, p. 974.
8. Shobha De, *Second Thoughts* (New Delhi, 1996), p. 259.
9. Shobha De, *Shooting from the Hip* (New Delhi, 1996), p. 110.
10. Jaydipsinh Dodiya, *The Fiction of Shobha De* (New Delhi: Prestige, 2000), p. 35.
11. *Ibid.*, p. 36.

The Feminist Stance: Rejection of Traditional Woman

In her novels, De's stance is the same taken by the feminists against those customs and norms of the society which place women in a position inferior to that of man—physically, politically, socially and economically. The feminist perspective has gained prominence ever since such women writers as Anita Desai, Nayantara Sahgal and Shobha De began to treat women's issues in their works and focused on the cause of the Indian women. A variety of shades of women's mind and plight is reflected in the writings of these women writers. In these novels there is the theme of rebellion against the social set up by its women characters. Women are no longer portrayed in the traditional mould where they are just identified as meek, weak and submissive creatures. These writers have created women protagonists who realize that they too have their own individual likes and dislikes. They want their voice to be heard in the society. Whether the voices of these women are received by attentive or deaf ears is not what matters. What, indeed, matters is that a new class of women has come up which is ready to take on the world to promote the women's perspective.

Women in the novels of Nayantara Sahgal are liberal and unconventional—Saroj in *Storm in Chandigarh* refuses to subscribe to meek, sober feminine behaviour as a socially acceptable norm. She longs to establish herself as an individual whereas for her husband, Inder, she is a mere wife. A woman's longing for love and understanding is convincingly depicted in the novel. Her husband keeps on pestering her with questions about her pre-marital affair with a boy. Inder wants Saroj to be a pious traditional wife while he asserts his male privilege by indulging in an extra-marital affair with Maya who is also a much-married woman. Saroj leaves her husband's house in protest against his cruel attitude towards her.

In Sahgal's other novels, *The Day in Shadow* and *Rich Like Us*, the women characters are seen revolting against male supremacy. Simrit in *The Day in Shadow* shows the plight of the Indian woman who fights her way out of her unhappy marriage. After she becomes a divorcee, she faces difficulties as the society looks upon her with cold eyes and malice. She has a tough time in almost all spheres of life—moral, social and economic.

Again, in Sahgal's *Rich Like Us* the heroine Shonali despite occupying an affluent and highly responsible post as an I.A.S. officer finds it difficult to avoid marriage. Marriage and its inevitability in our conservative society is given a new look. Getting married seems to be the final goal of a woman. Again, to be a woman entails facing various types of difficulties even if she is the boss in her office. The male officials who are not used to obeying a woman at home find a female boss in the office hard to digest.

Nayantara Sahgal's women are the new women who want freedom from all social and moral obligations which bind an Indian woman hard and fast. They fight against male dominance. Whether they ultimately win or not is not important; they demonstrate that they have in them the spirit of rebellion and not the conventional impulse for submission. Nayantara Sahgal's women are "strivers and aspirers, toward freedom, toward goodness, toward a compassionate world. Their virtue is a quality of heart and mind and spirit, a kind of untouched innocence and integrity."[1]

In Anita Desai's novels also the feminist standpoint is manifest even though her revolting women characters are rather weak. Yet they are unwilling to accept the female subjugation syndrome of Indian society. Her novels *Cry, the Peacock* and *Voices in the City* show their leading women protagonists Maya and Monisha rebel against their insensitive and unfeeling husbands who never so much as bother to know how their wives were going on with their lives.

Maya's image as a rebellious woman is the result of the frustration of her wifely aspirations. She yearns for her husband Gautama's love and needs him to satisfy both her physical and emotional needs. But her husband flees from her love. He has a strong tendency to recoil from any physical nearness. He never shows any understanding of his wife's feelings. As an educated modern woman Maya finds it unacceptable to silently bear Gautama's indifference towards her. She feels outraged at his indifference towards her existence. As such she develops a psychological problem which turns her desire for love into hatred of Gautama. At its climax, in a fit of extreme anger, she kills him and also kills herself.

In *Voices in the City*, Desai again shows the pathetic plight of Monisha, an educated young woman married in a conservative middle class joint family. She hates the monotony of traditional housewives whose minds are always preoccupied with such things as saris, jewellery and babies. Monisha finds her home environment repelling for there is nothing to give her a feeling that she too has her individuality. Her husband Jiban cannot reciprocate her love and can scarcely realize her pain. She is accused of stealing a small amount of her husband's money that she had paid to clear the hospital bill of her ailing younger brother. That strikes the final blow to her already shrinking existence that finally leads her to commit suicide. She resorts to suicide as the only means to release herself from her sorrow and pain.

Anita Desai's women revolt against the traditional submissive Sati-Savitri types who silently accept their fate as suppressed individuals. Desai's women come to realize that a woman's need is not for silent acceptance but a rejection of the rules of the family and the indifference of the husband. Both Maya and Monisha rebel even though their approach to life is pessimistic and cowardly as both of them commit suicide.

Therefore, the recurring theme of Anita Desai's novels is the woman's feeling of agony of existence in a male-dominated society that is unjust to women and that imposes various kinds of restraints on them. As a result of these restraints, their freedom of speech and action is curbed. They lose their sense of participation in life and suffer a sense of insecurity in their lives. They live but suffer from a feeling of loneliness and become introverts. Despondency, failures and frustrations limit their human relationships within and outside the family. On the other hand, "we perceive the struggles of the protagonists as heroic attempts that finally bring glory to the individual and add dignity to the spirit of freedom."[2]

The advocacy of women's problems is clearly seen in the works of Indian women novelists. What was just a beginning in writers like Anita Desai and Nayantara Sahgal gets a more strident treatment in Shobha De and other women novelists.

Shobha De strikes the latest trend in her feminist stance—that is, to reject outright the male hegemony. She is totally different from other Indian women writers. Her writings constitute a strong literary bashing of the Indian male. Through her novels she tries to shatter the unsympathetic and uncivilized attitude of callousness and indifference of men towards women.

In De's novels the women characters take all decisions and appear to be the masters of their own lives. These women are no soft and weak creatures who are frequently under the power of men and society. These women are set in the rich aristocratic society of Mumbai. They are independent, confident and assertive. They form that class of women who are trendsetters. The future generations of women will follow their footsteps and look at them as pioneers.

In our still conservative Indian society, the coming of this class of new women has attracted a lot of attention. Their life-style is very intriguing and tempting to any middle class educated urban woman. The new woman is a free individual. She is adorned in a different way with different ideas and values. She takes on her male counterpart with ease and confidence and sends a clear message to him that she is not a plaything but his tough competitor and an equal partner in any enterprise. The women of her type usually take up professions which are glamorous as well as highly challenging—professions such as advertising, journalism, acting, modelling and even big business. They live life on the fast tract. They are no husband worshippers, nor is marriage the most priced relationship for them. For them even social acceptance and recognition of any action of theirs is not a necessary requirement for succeeding in life. Whatever they do, they do so merely to satisfy their own selves. To these women life is not something that demands silent submission but a challenge to be boldly accepted and met.

In De's works there is a clear picture of the new woman's unconventional outlook on life. This new woman is out to grapple for equal power with man. As De observes:

> Eventually, every relationship is a power struggle either on an overt or subliminal level . . . control over the situation has been a male prerogative over the centuries. Women's destinies have been determined largely in that context alone . . . It is time they were made aware of their own potential and power. Shakti needs to be harnessed, directed and explored for the furtherance of overall human development. The very concept of sexes locked in eternal battle is negative and destructive. When one talks of shakti unleashed, one also remembers the two connotations of shakti . . . the destructive avtaar is as potent as the creative one. It is in maintaining the state of equilibrium between these two opposing forces that leads to creative and dynamic harmony. . . . Men will have to come to terms with woman power.[3]

De emphasizes the need for recognition of equivalence of power between men and women. In her novels male hierarchy is no longer the chief principle. Man's prerogative to lead life as he pleases has lapsed. Women in her novels are powerful enough to decide what is best for them. They do not accept any male interference in their affairs.

In her novel *Sisters*, the protagonist Mallika Hiralal makes her stand very clear when she takes over the charge of Hiralal industries after her father's death. She intends to run the industries on her own terms. She does not need any advice of anybody, not even of Ramankaka who was a close confidant of her father who now offers his help in the management of her business. Acknowledging his help, she firmly and confidently brushes him aside:

> Thank you for your advice Ramankaka, I appreciate and value your words. But I'd like you to hear a few of mine now. I can't change my sex, unfortunately. . . . But I can change just about everything else . . . and I intend to. . . . This is going to be my show and I intend running it on my terms. If the old solicitors aren't prepared to talk turkey with me, I will sack them. That goes for the accountants and anybody else who wishes to treat me like a simple-minded spoilt little girl out to play being a business woman. My genes are the same as my father's even if my gender isn't.[4]

These authoritative words of Mikki challenge the age-old concept of Indian society that treats a girl's business acumen as worthless and hence not dependable. Mikki is able to show her determination to take full control of the huge industry on her young shoulders and she is all out to punish those presumptuous male officials who try to display the usual air of superiority to her. Against the conventional attitude of males it is no doubt a tough job for a woman to be the boss in such a big business empire. Yet, Mikki is confident and undeterred in the resolve to carry on with the task of managing the business. In a patriarchal male-dominated society it is usually the man who exercises all power and it is under his guidance and directions that a woman is expected to act and follow. De's women follow a completely opposite life-style. They show sufficient will power to challenge, defy and retaliate whenever they get a feeling of being subdued by men.

Women belonging to this new clan do not take marriage as sacrosanct; it happens because it is convenient to them. The tradition-bound women regard marriage as a sacred bond which they strive to uphold in the face of all odds and sufferings. Once married, a woman is expected to be loyal to her husband, while for the husband it is his pleasure whether to honour the marriage or break it or play with. A man can loiter around with a number of mistresses while the woman has to sulk silently at home with all the hurt and humiliation. If a woman happens to have a secret relationship after marriage, she will be socially and within the family ostracized as characterless. The image of the new woman in De's novels thus turns the tables upside down. Her women launch an assault against the conservative tradition of moral values which bind them from rebelling. De's women have a number of boy friends as much as their husbands have girl friends. In *Socialite Evenings*, Karuna the protagonist shares a passionate relationship with her husband's friend Krish. Instead of keeping it a secret she is open about it. She tells her husband:

> There's no point in post mortems. I don't believe in them. Let's get on with the story. I love this friend of yours, and I want to be with him—in Venice. There is a good chance that I will feel thoroughly disillusioned after that. Maybe he will have some truly foul personal habits that will disenchant me. In which case it will be A Death in Venice. You know by now that I'm steady and grounded. It's the Taurean in me that's surfacing these days. Treat this as a short term mania that will wear itself out—and then we can go back to business as usual.[5]

Again, Karuna's friend and mentor Anjali also has a string of lovers like her husband Abbas who leads a reckless, promiscuous life. Anjali renounces her marriage for she is tired of

Abbas's humiliating behaviour towards her. She feels humiliated for being displaced from her own bedroom whenever Abbas's guests decide to stay with them for the night after the party. The divorce happens without any hassles which gives Anjali full freedom in carrying on with her affairs unhindered. Finally, she marries Kumar who has enormous wealth but is a homosexual who fulfils his sexual lust with a young boy Murty.

Anjali marries Kumar for all the wrong reasons. She had earlier married him for his wealth and social standing. Finding no satisfaction in marriage she opts for a divorce. Karuna as well as the other women in the novel feel the same way:

> We treated marriage like a skin allergy—an irritant all right, but not something that would incapacitate us. We had our own secret lives—and by that I do not mean clandestine affairs. But these are our private worlds, inaccessible to the men we had married. I could spend hours in this world, even when the husband was around talking to me. There was thrill in switching off and pretending to be there listening while being lost in a universe created by me, for myself. (46)

In De's *Sisters*, Mallika marries Binny Malhotra to save her father's failing business rather than for her liking. As her friend Amy had advised her:

> The quickest way to shoot to the top is tie up with Malhotra. And I am being practical when I tell you this—what's the worst thing that could happen in that alliance? A disastrous marriage can always be put behind you darling. These days divorce isn't what it used to be. You are young and attractive. There will be dozens of Malhotras later. You need a knight, even in tarnished armour right now. (465)

In De's *Snapshots*, all the six women have diverse marital status. Reema and Surekha had arranged marriage and they were lucky enough to get the best catches from the marriage market which is wildly competitive. Rashmi is an unwed mother who has to work to look after her son after his irresponsible father had left her high and dry. Swati and Aparna are divorcees. Noor is still single and unmarried.

That being the manner in which the marriages are made and broken, the feminists tend to devalue the institution of marriage. Marriage is no longer regarded as an essential element for the well-being of the family and society in De's novels. Marriages are no longer considered to be made in heaven. Educated and attractive, confident and assertive, this new class of women has given marriage a new meaning because of the absence of mutual faithfulness between husband and wife. Due to the husband's betrayal the woman claims her right to enjoy unlimited sexual freedom. Constancy and faithfulness in their married lives seem to be bygone values and no longer relevant. Like Reema who says very freely in *Snapshots*: "Imagine not knowing any body, any other feeling, any other sensation. Forever, sounds terrible. Like eating dal-chaval day in and day out!"[6]

The age-old dominance of the male in sexual matters is overthrown and rejected. The new women unequivocally come out with bold statements and actions dethroning such male prerogatives.

The new woman is out to carve out an identity of her own. She is little willing to live within the four walls of the house. She wants to move out of it and explore new horizons. She ventures to take up high-flying, well-paid jobs. Until recently a woman however well-educated she might have been had to be content with socially acceptable jobs like teaching, medicine, law, etc. But now her job preferences have changed. De's women are in modelling, films, advertising, journalism, business, etc. It is unthinkable for any tradition-bound woman to step out of the house at odd hours of the day to keep film shooting assignments or to collect news items if she happens to be a journalist. People may still be conservative and wag their tongues at seeing energetic young women join any similar fast tract assignments. Karuna in *Socialite Evenings* meets with grave objections from her family, especially from her father, when she opts for modelling:

> Father flashed the newspaper in front of me. 'When did you do this? How dare you? Do you mean to disgrace us completely? This is not something girls from respectable families do. . . .' A smile must have appeared on my face, because suddenly I felt Father's palm hitting me sharply across the face. (14)

Yet, instead of relenting and changing her mind, Karuna goes ahead with her ambitious assignment until she achieves a name as a famous model. She walks her way despite strong objections from her parents. In *Starry Nights*, Aasha Rani becomes a well-known film actress but she has to shed all her girlish shyness and flaunt her body in order to get a break in the Hindi film industry. The question of moral values is not even thought of. Aasha Rani uses her body as a bait to catch the attention of the film directors and producers. To obtain money and fame she stops at nothing, not even in losing her virginity. Amrita in *Strange Obsession* also dares to stay all alone in a city like Mumbai, far from home, to pursue her career as a model. She is ready to overcome any obstacles in embracing the fast life of this city. She is so sure of herself that when she lands herself in the company of the lesbian Minx, she does not regret her decision nor does she think of going back to her parents. She carries on with her job and puts up with Minx's amorous advances. For this woman too her career, fame and money matter more than anything else.

In *Sisters* too, Mikki Hiralal and Alisha Hiralal are highly ambitious and headstrong women who jump into the competitive world of high level business. Mikki's handling of her father's huge business empire after his death is remarkable. It is a tough job for a young fragile woman like her to become a business tycoon, but she accepts the challenge and succeeds. In the words of the novelist herself: "Mallika Hiralal was all set to make her own way into the corporate world as the undisputed queen of a cluster of companies her father had built from scratch." (421)

Later when her husband Binny Malhotra stops her from pursuing her career after their marriage, Mikki feels hurt and humiliated. But after Binny's sudden death in an accident, she takes time by the forelock and gets back on her job.

The new woman does not consider it her responsibility to stick around home taking care of the husband's needs and looking after the kids. Nisha in *Sultry Days* describes the new woman:

> These were no-nonsense women who had 'take me seriously' written all over them. They even wore business suits to work and carried burgundy coloured briefcases. . . . Their male colleagues were not permitted to crack jokes or flirt lightly. . . . Workaholism for women had become very fashionable. "If men can pursue career ruthlessly, so can we," women declared at seminars and workshops for senior managers. . . . The poor husbands were caught entirely unprepared.[7]

These women break the general social rules which keep them under the supremacy of males. They are anxious to establish their separate, individual identity. They are not happy to be recognized as the wives of Mr. so and so. They crave for their own space and achieve it in the face of all odds. The feminists are involved in evoking in them the consciousness, the new reality of their right to equality with man. The De novels certainly go a long way in projecting that feminist stance.

As per the new reality, men are regarded as partners of convenience and not of obligation by women. These women don't consider man as an important element in their lives. They need and use man as a ladder to wealth and status. Karuna in *Socialite Evenings* never treats her husband as her partner deserving due attention and care. His presence is minimized as much as possible. The name of the husband is not revealed throughout the novel; only the word 'He' is used to refer to him. Karuna's marriage with him is merely to give her a ticket to push herself into the high social circle of Mumbai. As she says: "maybe I accepted the marriage, sans passion, sans anything, because it suited me. I didn't have to exert myself. I didn't have to prove anything. He seemed grateful enough for my presence." (44) She further adds sarcastically: "Poor fools . . . they were simple and uncomplicated and, therefore, happy creatures." (45)

After Karuna's divorcing her husband she makes acquaintances with a number of guys in the process of building her career. But at no time does she show any anxiety to marry again. Instead she keeps those guys at the level of friends only despite several proposals for remarriage extended by them. Her mother's pressure on her to remarry meets with a cold reply:

> But mother, why does security rest with a man? I feel confident now that I look after myself. I am earning as much as any man. I have a roof over my head. I don't really have any responsibilities. I am at peace with myself. I'm not answerable to anyone, I don't feel like complicating my life, by getting into a second marriage. (201)

Karuna is so self-confident that her single status can make her life more enterprising and much more happy. It looks as if she puts the marital relationship in cold storage, making the male partner an unnecessary encumbrance.

The image of man that emerges from Shobha De's novels is generally negative. A male character is frequently portrayed as a seducer, exploiter, wife-beater, rapist, torturer or a cruel, callous husband. In *Starry Nights*, Aasha Rani's father is a case in point. She cannot forget his shameful act of deserting her mother. He is regarded as a filthy womanizer. Aasha Rani recollects: "Piecing amma's life together, Aasha Rani knows more or less of what had happened. How appa had lost interest in her? How Girija had humiliated her and called her a common prostitute. How appa abruptly cut off all money. . . . That was when the nightmare had begun. Moving out of their luxurious bungalow and into some ugly little place in an over-crowded filthy area."[8] Aasha Rani's mother was left to fend for herself and her two daughters. She was broke and home-less.

In *Sisters* too, Mikki after her marriage finds her husband Binny a cruel, unfeeling male who had no consideration for her feelings. When Mikki tells him about her pregnancy he becomes wild with rage. Mikki narrates the sad incident to her friend Amy: "When she finally did . . . he exploded. She'd thought he was going to hit her. Next morning, he told me to arrange for an abortion. When I refused he said it was that or a divorce." (493)

Binny's ill-treatment of Mikki in their married life ex-poses the contrast between the pre-marriage falsehood of man's behaviour and the truth of post-marital behaviour in which his real self comes out. In her novels De brings out the reality of true nature of the Indian males.

De's feminist stance helps her to elaborate upon the atti-tude of conservative Indians with regard to the not openly dis-cussed topic of sex. In her novels sex is deliberately and openly flaunted and discussed. It is something that needs to be openly discussed and not made a private secret.

According to De, all people need sex. It is something spe-cial, something beautiful, something shared. The new woman highlights sex on her own terms. "The very fact," she adds, "that sex is no longer the most dreaded and despised three-letter word in India is enough cause to celebrate."[9] But there is nothing derogatory in clandestine sex. In fact, sex is "the bed-rock of all relationships."[10]

The feminists have exploded the myth of secrecy about sex. Men have been keeping it a secret but the new woman has boldly exposed it and opened it for discussion. Its con-cealment had perhaps made her weak, and its exposure has given her a new strength and superiority over man undreamed of before. All the women characters in De's novels are conscious of the importance of sex in their lives. While they enjoy sex to fulfil their own passion, at the same time they use it as a weapon against men to keep them under their control. Outside fiction, it is still unthinkable for the modern Indian females to show off their desire for sex. But in the case of De's women they freely talk and indulge in sexuality. Karuna in *Socialite Evenings* says: "Men like dogs could be conditioned through reward and punishment." (60) Her use of the strategy of reward and punishment clearly hints that a woman can withdraw from man according to her requirement or liking. De rejects all notions of respectability associated with marriage. Her women discuss and enjoy sex without restraint. In *Starry Nights*, Rita advises Malini, the dejected angry wife of the famous film actor Akshay Arora on how to keep her husband in her grip:

> Romance finishes the morning after the wedding night. After that what? Boredom. Men like variety. We women have to put up with that and switch our minds to something else. . . . All wives have to pretend. Just shut your eyes and part your legs. But I am telling you act, act, act, that's what she has to do. Everything is decided by the bed. On the bed. (265)

Here, Rita emphasizes on the need of compromise in sustaining marital relationships. She even feels that to pretend is the best way to keep a marriage going.

In *Snapshots*, Rashmi feels that sex is a matter of "mutual need and mutual dependency." (906) She further says, "Mediocre women used sex as bait or food. It was the shrewd ones who used their brain. And schemed throughout their lives to hold their men, keep them enslaved." (907) Swati the most daring of all six friends in the novel freely comments on sex, pointing to the strong stance of the new woman on the subject: "Sex isn't filthy . . . our minds make it so. Look at Khajuraho, Konark . . . have any of you studied the *Kama Sutra*? Fascinating. It's a pity we got brainwashed by some frustrated, repressed idiots. I think sex is a celebration—the highest form of religion." (979)

Referring to India, De underlines the eroticism in India's renowned art and sculpture. In the past India nurtured liberal thinkers on sex, namely, Kalidas, Jayadip, Vidyapati and more recently Rajneesh. Even the present-day world extols the erotic art of Khajuraho and Konark. And India takes pride in these artistic monuments. Obviously, sex is prurient only to those who possess a repressed sensibility and a prurient mind.[11]

De demonstrates a maturer attitude towards sex. In conclusion, it is to be noted that Shobha De has created the new woman who is daring and fearless. She has consciously created characters and themes to draw attention to the different kinds of repression and exploitation of women in India. She is not bothered about her language or aesthetics in her writings. She has thus joined the host of feminists in exposing the women's situation and underlining the need for recognition of the new woman's power and superiority which had been suppressed in the past. This is the new realism which is steadily coming up in urban Indian high society, where women are no longer slaves of men physically and financially, where men are finding the new woman giving them complexes with her sharp brain and no-nonsense attitude. De has given a full throated message in her novels that no man should underestimate women and that the new woman is here to stay and men beware of the new reality.

NOTES

1. K. Meera Bai, "Tradition and Modernity: The Portrayal of Women by Women Writers," *Indian Women Novelists*, ed. R.K. Dhawan (New Delhi, 1991), Vol. I, p. 41.
2. R.K. Dhawan, "Introduction: Indian Women Novelists," *Ibid.*, pp. 12-13.

3. Shobha De, *Shooting from the Hip: Selected Writings* (New Delhi, 1996), p. 111.
4. Shobha De, *Sisters*, in *Shobha De Omnibus* (New Delhi, 1995), p. 430.
5. Shobha De, *Socialite Evenings*, in *Shobha De Omnibus*, p. 135.
6. Shobha De, *Snapshots*, in *Shobha De Omnibus*, p. 969.
7. Shobha De, *Sultry Days*, in *Shobha De Omnibus*, p. 792.
8. Shobha De, *Starry Nights*, in *Shobha De Omnibus*, p. 279.
9. R.S. Pathak, "Feminist Concerns in Shobha De's Works: A Study in Attitude," in Jaydipsinh Dodiya, ed., *The Fiction of Shobha De* (New Delhi, 2000), p. 41.
10. *Loc. cit.*
11. *Ibid.*, p. 43.

A Critical Assessment of De as a Novelist: Contribution to Indian English Novel

After analyzing Shobha De's novels and other works, it wouldn't be wrong to say that she has done a marvellous job as a skilled feminist writer. De has been able to throw significant light on the inner life of men and women belonging to the glittering world of affluent sections of Indian society based mainly in Mumbai and on the new woman who now occupies the centrestage in this society. De's intimate knowledge of this circle by virtue of her being perhaps a member of this section has made it viable for her to bring out every little secret of this new woman out of the closet and present her as realistically as possible. To the young educated urban reader De's novels are a terrific combination of truthful, fearless and realistic writing, and the most alluring and entertaining studies of the high life of women and men belonging to this circle.

With *Socialite Evenings* (1989), De made her presence felt in a big way as the novel became a best-seller, "initially selling 3,000 copies. It is still in demand with sales now totalling 40,000."[1] It is indeed a record figure by Indian standards where English language novels sell in small number compared to the sales figures in other countries. Yet *Socialite Evenings* was labelled as a "high society pot pourri, and voyeuristic servings of souped-up, four-wheel drive-sex-in-all directions."[2]

No doubt, De has been a controversial writer throughout because her novels contain explicit sex scenes. When her second novel *Starry Nights* came out, a lot of unpleasant remarks came mostly from male reviewers. "Porn again De," declared one headline; "Queen of Quickies," cried another. That same year, an international magazine dubbed her the "Jackie Collins of India."[3] This remark was enough to attract readers outside India.

By laying bare the details of possibly real happenings in the world of the affluent, the self-sufficient new woman and her reckless sexual escapades and her various unfeminine attitudes, Shobha De projects the world of the new woman. It is only natural that as a literary writer she presents an honest and truthful image of this unconventional and even convention-bashing woman who aspires to subvert the male-dominated society. Consequently, her candid writings have got her into a generous amount of controversies. However, controversies have always cropped up whenever a writer writes freely about sex in his works. D.H. Lawrence's *Lady Chaterley's Lover*[4] was even taken to court for the element of promiscuity in it. Yet, he was acquitted as the novel only presented the shocking reality of the society which had always made sex a closely guarded subject of discussion. However, with the passage of time it was recognized that a writer is free to write whatever he wants, as his work becomes an eye-opener to the general public and makes it better educated in this matter. Treating sex as an untouchable or taboo topic only makes matters worse.

Like De, Salman Rushdie too has presented the sex theme in his novels the way women are subjected to physical as well as mental suffering and the unfavourable situation of women in the Islamic society. Rushdie still faces a death sentence or Fatwa pronounced by the Muslim fundamentalist leader Khomeni. He had to run for asylum in England. Another top woman writer of India, Mridula Garg, became very controversial for writing about sex in her novel *Chitcobra*. "Till a few decades ago such writings were still done by women at their own peril as male censure was prevalent. After its publication in the Seventies, Garg was arrested and charged under the Obscenities Act. Her crime: she highlighted the female protagonist as *Pryagya-rupa* (aware woman) as opposed to just *Matri-rupa* and *Priya-rupa* (mother and lover). The book delineated a thinking woman's dichotomy between the body and mind while making love to her husband."[5]

It may be noted that sex has become an internationally accepted and celebrated topic in literature. Arundhati Roy's *The God of Small Things* which too touches upon the subject of sex was awarded the prestigious Booker Prize. Literary critics opine that Arundhati Roy's sexually explicit materials in the novel do not in any way harm or egregiously offend one's sense of morality since it constitutes erotic pornography and not thematic pornography. It depicts sexual relationship between two fully consenting (though not equal) partners Ammu and Velutha who emotionally identify with each other and treat each other as fully human persons. Such descriptions do not harm or degrade women or in any way promote sexual harassment, rape and woman battering since these descriptions, to the novelists, are related to the 'Small Things' of life—"the balls, the breast and the soft dark triangle."

Arundhati Roy dwells on, and lifts, the socially banned sexual expression into the realm of fun, frolic and romance through her poetic prose. She depicts good sex, "vanilla sex—that is gentle, touchy—freely side by side." In this sense it would not be wrong to call *The God of Small Things* effective writing that projects a powerful image of sexual experience within a social framework. "Arundhati Roy's *The God of Small Things* can aptly be called the novelist's projection of her sexist vision to be surveyed and appreciated by the male world."[6]

Likewise, Shobha De's presentation of sex in her novels is very liberal and convincing. It should be viewed as an eye-opener to the conservative Indian masses. Keeping sex under wraps would only breed more promiscuity. It is much better in being projected loud and clear so that everyone becomes aware of its power, so that every one is aware of its shortcoming if it is given a free play in the society.

What makes De a writer who is in great demand is her masterly art of story telling and yet putting in slices of factual reality in her novels. There is a clear voice of a feminist in her writings though De sometimes deviates from supporting the overtly developed new woman. She indirectly focuses on the unsavoury and unhealthy aspects of the character of a new woman. While on the one hand she lashes out at the Indian males by delineating their unwelcome behaviour and psyche, on the other hand she satirically exposes the emptiness in the lives of thsse new women who are obsessed with their precious diamonds and sexuality. Focussing on the main theme of the emergence of the new woman and despite the different unpleasant controversies evoked by her writings, De's novels present a totally new outlook on the women's world. In her fearless presentation of men and women living a high life, there is assuredly a deep moral purpose beneath their surface.

In the first chapter, "Shobha De: Life and Works," I have discussed Shobha De's background of belonging to an educated middle class home and later joining the league of the rich and the famous after her successful stint as a model, followed by a career in journalism and as a fiery editor of "popular magazines like *Stardust*, *Celebrity* and *Society*."[7] Shobha De had experienced life as a member of a conservative middle class under the strict guardianship of her bureaucrat father. She had fought her way out of the conservative home environment to make her mark in the high life of Mumbai, in which she succeeded despite all odds. Throughout her novels as she pens down the lives of the high society women, she has shown the new face of the totally, emancipated woman with all her daring adventures and deeds. She unravels the psyche of these characters in order to show how the changes in their behaviour come about and how far the changes have been rewarding and also at the same time tending to destroy the softer, mellower feminine quality of these women which is contrary to what is associated with the behaviour of the womankind.

De's own experience of the high society gave her the impetus to write some of the dazzling novels—*Socialite Evenings*, *Starry Nights*, *Sisters*, *Strange Obsession*, *Sultry Days*, *Snapshots* and *Second Thoughts*. These novels are set in the glittering backdrop of Mumbai's social circle where men and women lead luxurious but reckless lives, throwing away all traditional and moral inhibitions of the conservative Indian society. Her women are obsessed with aspiration for wealth, power and fame. They acquire an image which is in contrast to the image of the traditional Indian women who devote their lifetime in the service of their husbands and family. Extra-marital affairs are unthinkable to these traditional women even if their husbands keep several mistresses. They feel that it is men's inherent right to have any number of wives while a woman has no right to such relationships for if she does she will be shunned and dubbed as characterless. These women have no voice of their own. They feel that whatever men and society tell them to do, it is their sole duty to obey unquestioningly. Consequently, they suffer innumerable injustices in all walks of life. Even women who are born in the modern age and have full awareness of the new voice of women's emancipation will still find themselves influenced by the traditional customary practices of the male-dominated society. A number of well-educated women who could have gone out on their own and made careers for themselves have to sit back at home when the family is conservative and disapproves of their working outside the premises of their homes. Women still occupy a very lowly position in our society despite the fact that it is now the dawn of the twenty-first century. The new century should create a new awakening in the men and make them realize that the new age demands that they should accord due recognition to women as equal partners in all walks of life, welcome them to take part in decision-making in all affairs inside and outside the family matters, a new life which is lived in mutual cooperation and mutual respect for each other. While this is the demand and spirit of the new age, the shades of the old spirit and values of life have not yet given way to the new values. Promises of the new spirit are yet words merely on paper and not fully translated into reality.

What is, in fact, visible is a kind of rebellion against the old culture with the emergence of a breed of new women from the upper class of Indian society which challenges men's hierarchy in every sphere of life. These women are highly challenging, educated and assertive. They are out to tell men that whatever they do, they too are entitled to do the same. They go in for high flying careers like modelling, movies, high power business, journalism and advertising. They keep a string of men tied under their belts, so that when one fails to live up to their expectations, they can move on to the next one. Men are expected to satisfy their carnal desires and give them social status. To them a marriage is a formality and a matter of personal convenience. If that purpose is not served by marriage they do not hesitate to cast it away and clean their path of undesired obstacles. Morality is what suits them. The conventional morality is thrown to the winds for in the morals of these new women, nothing is immoral. In fact, what they do is absolutely justified and nobody has a right to poke their nose into it. In the process of doing whatever they like, they become victims of their own recklessness. A number of women become wildly self-obsessed. They forget that by their wild life-style, their own young children's lives become highly vulnerable to a reckless life-style, hazarding too much preoccupation with sex, money, violence and drugs. In the backdrop of this value-pattern De sets her novels and each novel presents a captivating image of the actual lives of the attractive high society women with all their power and weaknesses.

In 1997, an article entitled "Feminist New Style" in *Harper's Magazine* declared the newly-evolved modern to be a composite figure, a boyish girl who combines the flapper's physical freedom, sexuality and stamina with feminist self-assertiveness and traditional domestic feminity, a woman who can happily combine pleasure, career and marriage. To the advanced young man of the time, this new woman seems the perfect companion—fearless, bright and eager to participate in work, in play, in marital sex. We know this image might be admired but not easily accepted by the Indian males. Shobha De, however, shapes her women in the above frame.[8]

In the second chapter I have analyzed the image of the traditional woman versus that of the new, modern woman. Tradition no longer commands respect with these new women. All De's women characters from Karuna in *Socialite Evenings* to Maya in *Second Thoughts* determinedly defy tradition in order to fulfil their desires and dreams. The tendency to look deep into life is pervasive in the characters of these novels. It gives the women characters a new urge and a power to shake off and defy male supremacy in all spheres of life. They are successful, rich and highly individualistic. Karuna easily walks out of her marriage once she finds herself ill-adjusted in her home. She finds her husband a cold, conservative dull male, like any other Indian male. She looks for a man who can understand her feelings and sentiments, someone who will allow her to be her own self without any compulsion. De's women characters' search for independence makes them fiercely career-oriented unlike the traditional women who always rely on men for all kinds of moral and economic support. They earn enough to sustain themselves and stand by their own strength without any support from any man. Sometimes they become the guardians of their own homes as single mothers who raise their siblings after their broken marriages This is to be seen particularly in her novel *Snapshots*:

> Rashmi sighed, holding the boy close to her. So much like her father, she thought. Stubborn, headstrong and impetuous—and talented. Even she had to admit as much. Strange that he should be a mini-replica of Pips Sr., the brilliant movies director who'd walked out on her when she was pregnant with Pips. Walked out. Just like that.[9]

The actress Aasha Rani in *Starry Nights* also ends up as a single mother after her divorce from her husband. Both Aasha Rani and Karuna take up the responsibility of looking after aging parents and take care of the financial requirements of their families.

The financial independence in turn makes these women so very self-assured and confident that they can take care of their own needs as well as of the family members. Their exposure to the high social circle induces in them a desire to enjoy the same freedom and fun as are enjoyed by the women of that circle and strengthens their resolve to decide for themselves what suits their interest most. A man becomes only a necessary tool to achieve their goals. These women aspire for everything that gives them power and equal footing with men. They are ready to make every compromise till they can attain their desired goals.

De uses her writing talent deftly to pinpoint the wide gulf between the new woman and the traditional woman who are at opposite ends of the scale and can never reconcile with one another. This difference between tradition and modernity is clearly seen in the following conversation of Karuna and her mother:

> "I'm not doing this as a profession. It is only a hobby." "What sort of a hobby is this. I've not come across such a hobby before. In our time girls learned how to cook, knit, crochet, embroider, make rangolis. We called such activities hobbies. Yes, a few girls these days collect stamps or learn drawing. But what you are doing is not hobby." "I enjoy it, and I have not done anything wrong." "That is what you think. Once parents allow girls to slip out of their control

> then everything goes wrong. We don't want that to happen to you."[10]

The traditional woman is a meek, weak woman who will forever live in the shadow of man bearing solidly all the atrocities of the male-dominated society. On the contrary, the modern woman is a rebel who is aggressive enough and unprepared to be second to man. De's portrayal of the modern woman is awesome and even thought-provoking. She is engaged in showing how far these women go in their wild pursuit for realizing their aspirations and attaining a distinct identity.

While dealing with the serious subject-matter of their aesthetic perceptions of the new woman, questions relating to their morality naturally arise. One can say that De's women frequently display their aesthetic perceptions and preferences in different novels. De presents these while portraying the new women and the society in which they live. The new woman is an enigma. Her life style is impressive as well as intriguing to any eager middle class urban reader especially the women. De's language in the novels is not decorative but rather straightforward and blunt and even socially unrefined. It hits the nail right on the head. Whether it is the characters or their words everything creates a precise impact on the mind of the reader. By using a free transparent language Shobha De succeeds in making her point clear, the point that women need no longer be silent sufferers, that they have the potential for being fierce rebels capable of claiming their equal share in all things that a man enjoys, the share that was previously denied them. De's aesthetics lies in her ability to project the taste and temperament of the new women and present factual details as realistically as possible. By depicting their aesthetic perceptions, De underlines the new morality that these women believe in. In fact De's image of the new woman provides a glimpse of the new reality that woman's awakening can create if she is denied her legitimate rights and recognition by the male-dominated society.

From the plot outlines of all the seven novels of De it is also seen that these women are all violators of the age-old concept of traditional Indian morality. They have no hassles in going against the prevalent social and moral codes which allow them limited freedom and do not permit them to do certain things which the society regards as the exclusive domain of the males—such as choosing a career which requires working outside their homes, or most importantly divorcing their husbands as soon as they find their actions unacceptable or if they are unable to meet their biological and emotional demands.

A striking feature of the new woman is that she does not make morality a big issue. To her morality is a term that may mean different things to different people at different times. It can undergo change from time to time in tune with the changing values and demands of the new woman. To her working outside home and associating with male friends can no longer be regarded as immoral. She wants the society to take cognizance of the new conditions of life and working of the women in the competitive world of today which compel her to become forward-looking, educated and highly individualistic. Everything that these women do justifies their ideology.

An open discussion of a hitherto reserved subject such as sex is no longer a taboo. Women in the novels of De openly declare and discuss the need for sex in their lives. Like Swati says in *Snapshots*: "we rejoice in our sexuality. We don't suppress it. We don't dismiss it. We don't find it dirty. Sex doesn't threaten us. I'm not afraid to fuck. I feel sorry for all you women hanging on so desperately to outdated ideas of purity, morality, and chastity. It's pathetic." (977) These women indulge in a number of promiscuous, sexual adventures outside their marriage or even before marriage. The act of sex is not limited to the opposite sex but extends to females of the same sex too. Homosexuality and lesbianism find a firm root in the world of this rich society of well-established women. As long as the persons concerned are satisfied with these relationships, which no doubt appears strange in the eyes of the conservative common Indian, nothing else matters. These women may be called immoral by the conventional standards of morality but to them it is only the most justified form of sexual independence and not a matter of shame or disdain. This new morality is, therefore, a characteristic feature of the new woman's life.

Coming to the issue of realism in De's novels, it is found that De's characters and their life-styles are suggestive of the real life-styles of members of some upper sections of Indian society. These high society people are usually rich business tycoons, film industry people, politicians and underworld dons. They have money and power at their command and live reckless lives. In this society the women are shown as equally ruthless and powerful. Whatever the menfolk enjoy they demand the same. In fact, they make men dance to their tunes.

Aasha Rani in *Starry Nights*, Mikki and Alisha Hiralal in *Sisters*, Karuna in *Socialite Evenings*, Swati in *Snapshots* and Amrita in *Strange Obsession*—all of them use their husbands as means to fulfil their desires. They are established career women; for them the world is no longer the male domain alone but it is equally theirs as well in all matters. The new reality is that women are no longer dependent on men. There is a reversal of hierarchy and in place of men it is women who take care of the family and themselves without the necessity to have a man around. They exude a new confidence in themselves because of their financial strength: these women earn more than enough to meet all the needs of the family. Financial independence makes them feel that they no longer need the shoulders of a man to put their weight upon. As Karuna tells her mother: "But mother, why does security rest with a man? I feel confident now that I can look after myself. I am earning as much as any man. I have a roof over my head. I don't really have any responsibilities. I am at peace with myself. I'm not answerable to anyone. I don't feel like complicating my life by getting into a second marriage." (201)

They are capable enough to shoulder their responsibilities. The new reality is that they despise the feminine qualities of dependencee, meekness and passivity that characterized the traditional Indian woman.

In chapter five, the element of feminist stance in De's novels is distinctly brought out. De projects the image of the new woman who craves for equal status with man and fights the male hegemony with great zeal. These women are fighters and not silent acceptors of injustice and unfair treatment meted out to them by the patriarchal society. De's novels throw light on their capacity and determination to use men to satisfy their lust for money, fame and status as also to satiate their excessive sexual appetite. The feminist stance is so strongly given that it reduces man to insignificance. De's feminist stance may be one of the harshest messages given by women writers to patriarchal society.

De's novels emphasize that men should wash their minds clean of such an absurd notion as that women should be kept in a subordinate position at home and in the society. The indifference and callous attitude shown by man towards a woman's feelings and sentiments is responsible for the rise of the new woman. Tired of the male-centred culture, the new woman wants to bring about a radical transformation of the existing society so that women may have their own voice and respectability and enjoy equal rights with man. These women are highly educated and they want a free platform to show off their respective talents. They refuse to sacrifice their talents for the sake of keeping the marriage going. For these women marriage is a secondary element in their lives while a career and the fulfillment of other personal desires are given topmost priority. These women are of the firm belief that they can survive on their own without dependence on anyone. They are not bothered about social approval for they strongly abhor the male-centric social set-up which makes them vulnerable and easy prey to man's physical power. They reject the traditional social thinking that a woman's place is at the feet of her husband and his use of force to coerce her into obedience as valid, a practice still prevalent in both the higher and the lower sections of society. De's novels draw a clear feminist image of the emerging new woman who is not the man's shadow but his equal partner, a master of her own will and a force to reckon with.

In conclusion, it may be noted that De has been able to project a realistic image of the new woman in her novels and that the presentation is sufficiently thought-provoking in so far as it gives a positive moral message to our conservative patriarchal society. The moral message is that the age-old process of suppression of women cannot be held valid. On the contrary, an unsympathetic attitude toward women could inspire more evil in society and make them revolt at their inhuman treatment by making them like sacrificial animals at the altar of man's lust for power and sex.

There have also been times in history when great men like Ishwar Chandra Vidyasagar, Swami Vivekananda, Vinoba Bhave and others worked for the upliftment of Indian women. They embarked upon the programme of raising the standard of women in the conservative Indian society through their education and working towards their emancipation. As a result of their dedicated endeavours, the lot of women has improved. This can be clearly seen in the emergence of working women in various fields of development of the country. But despite various social changes women are still generally inclined to take up positions subordinate to men. This is still the trend even in the present times. However, with the rise of the new class of women who are exposed to the liberal and trendy attitude of the West and the European countries towards women via media and learning, many of them have become rebels against the conservative society. They aspire to acquire an identity of their own, and take seriously to feminist ways.

In her novels, De mostly concentrates on the upper middle section of women which seriously adheres to the western life-style. They constitute the affluent section of the middle and upper class. Men and women, who belong to the glittering social circle who wine and dine in luxury and promiscuity, are no doubt small in number. They are looked upon by the common people as celestial beings. The men and women belonging to this society are reckless creatures with a new set of social and moral values which will be seen as immoral by the general Indian masses.

De's presentation of the women belonging to this society is that of a rebel who does not conform either to tradition or to modernity but chooses to attain a different identity, whereby she may not have to follow any social or moral code of conduct. These women are too self-absorbed; they frequently go into a wild race for power and money which they may not always win. But by their conduct and persuasion they tempt the younger women to enter the same race and so lead the tradition-conscious women away from the softer and humbler path of womanliness.

It may however be noted that while presenting the colourful and glamorous image of the new woman and her outstanding achievements, De seems to be pointing also to the negative aspects of their achievement and aspirations. Her portrayals are very much true to life. Whatever she has created reflects the true image of the new woman and the society she lives in. With her realistic writings De has carved out a distinctive place for herself among the well-read women novelists of India. The individual women and a section of society that she portrays represents a miniscule of the larger society outside of her novels. Let it be firmly kept in mind by readers that her novels represent what Georg Lukács calls "artistically generated reflection"[17] of a section of the society and not the whole society as she found it around her.

The image of the new woman De has portrayed represents the type of women from the affluent sections of the high stratum of modern Indian society. These women are adequately self-dependent and well provided for and yet their behaviour calls for correction, for even their excessive freedom creates problems. De has focussed adequately on these new women and it is left to these women to decide what would be best for them, whether to change their way a little or to defy every moral code of the male-dominated society which they shun or spurn.

De's journalistic career has helped her to present Mumbai life as realistically as possible. She uses commonplace "Hinglish," colloquial conversational mixture of Hindi and English words, as a part of her technique to provide local colour realism in her novels. She uses the Hindi-English colloquial mixture generously to give a powerful rendering of Indian sensibility. Hindi words and expressions abound in her novels, e.g., "Lehenga, zari-bordered angavastrams sexy sanyasis"[11] "Jadu-tona,"[12] "Apni lifeline pe lao,"[13] "Ho gaye hai,"[14] "Bas, just one drink,"[15] "Maine Pyar Kiya."[16] With the use of these words De captures the real spirit of such amorous conversations in Hindi and makes her novels full-blooded depictions of contemporary situations. The best part of De's use of this blend of Hinglish colloquialism is that it helps in bringing about an easy grasp of her storyline and themes to her Indian readers as a lot of Hindi words have been inserted here and there.

The use of Hindi words in her narratives has in fact increased the vocabulary of the English language. Any foreign or non-Hindi knowing reader reading her novels will be prompted to probe into the meanings of Hindi words for understanding their implications and enrich the English language with more variety, almost like what English language did by incorporating words from French and other European languages in writing and speaking English. Shobha De is marvellous in her induction of Hindi words in her writings. But what is certainly significant is that the frequent introduction and use of Hindi words and colloquial expressions renders her male and women characters more and more characteristically and typically Indian. With the help of these expressions the situations of the characters become more country- or subcontinent-specific.

De's novels sell like hot cakes and this is ample proof that she has succeeded as a writer. It is not only her novels which have raised a wide circle of readers but also other works which include a collection of her columns in weekly news magazines she has been writing for over two decades. Her compiled anthology on sex has sold over a million copies world wide. Her recent works *Speedpost* and *Spouse* have earned her a great fame. English literature students in India are writing doctoral theses relating to women's issues in her novels. Her first three novels have been chosen as course material at the University of London's School of Oriental Studies. This further testifies to De's capability as a writer. There is also ample proof that she is recognized and not taken lightly in this country as well as abroad. As Alka Saxena has aptly observed: "her critics were surprised and sore to hear that *Starry Nights* was recently prescribed as a text book in Bombay University. But we should remember that *Starry Nights*, her second novel, was already on the prescribed list in a British University, before it formed a part of a paper on Popular Culture for third year B.A. English at Bombay University in 1995-96."[18]

Another critic, Janaki Ramchandra, correctly states, "You may love or hate her, but it is difficult to ignore her."[19] It may not therefore be wrong to say that Shobha De will long remain a celebrated name among the women writers of India. She is no doubt blunt and candid in her writing, yet she is widely accepted. She has a long way to go and we look forward to having more works from her pen.

NOTES

1. Ajay Singh, "Trouble with Men," *Asiaweek* (from the internet).
2. Madhu Jain, "Cat on a Cold Tin Roof," *India Today*, Oct. 15, 1989, p. 195.
3. Ajay Singh, "The Trouble with Men," *Asiaweek*.
4. D.H. Lawrence, *Lady Chatterly's Lover* (New Delhi, 1992)
5. Surabhi Khosla, "The New Age of Women Authors" (*The South-Asian.com*, Feb. 2002).
6. S.P. Swain, "Erotic Pornography and Sexuality: A Study of Arundhati Roy's *The God of Small Things*," *Indian Writings in English*, ed. Manmohan Bhatnagar, Vol. IV (New Delhi, 1999), pp. 104-5.
7. Jaydipsinh Dodiya and R.K. Dhawan, "The Fiction of Shobha De: An Introduction," *The Fiction of Shobha De*, ed. Jaydipsinh Dodiya (New Delhi, 2000), p. 13.
8. Cf. Pushp Lata, "A Protest against the Patriarchal in Shobha De's Words," *The Fiction of Shobha De*, ed. Jaydipsinh Dodiya, p. 63.
9. Shobha De, *Snapshots*, in *Shobha De Omnibus* (New Delhi, 1995), p. 899.
10. Shobha De, *Socialite Evenings*, in *Shobha De Omnibus*, p. 21.
11. *Ibid.*, p. 110.
12. *Ibid.*, p. 167.
13. Shobha De, *Starry Nights*, in *Shobha De Omnibus*, p. 269.
14. *Ibid.*, p. 307.
15. Shobha De, *Sisters*, in *Shobha De Omnibus*, p. 442.
16. Shobha De, *Snapshots*, in *Shobha De Omnibus*, p. 886.
17. Georg Lukács, "Approximation to Life in the Novel and the Play," *Sociology of Literature and Drama*, ed. Elizabeth and Tom Burns (Penguin, 1973).
18. Alka Saxena, "Second Thoughts: A Slice of Urban Life," *The Fiction of Shobha De*, ed. Jaydipsinh Dodiya, p. 259.
19. E. Satyanarayana, "The Dialectics of Self-Assertion: The Liberated Woman in *Sisters*," *Ibid.*, p. 211.

Bibliography

Primary Sources

Novels

Socialite Evenings (1989).

Starry Nights (1990).

Sisters (1992).

Strange Obsession (1992).

Sultry Days (1994).

Snapshots (1996).

Second Thoughts (1996).

Short Stories

Small Betrayals. New Delhi: UBS, 1995.

Books

Shooting from the Hip. New Delhi: UBS, 1996.

Surviving Men. New Delhi: Penguin, 1997.

Selective Memory. New Delhi: Penguin, 1998.

Speedpost. New Delhi: Penguin, 1999.

Other Writings

"Fidelity test, Indian style," *The Sexes, The Week*, 22 September, 2002.

"All about skin," *The Sexes, The Week*, 6 October, 2002.

"Steamy leaves," *The Sexes, The Week*. From website, www-google.com.

"Striking a New Balance," *The Sexes, The Week*, 25 August, 2002.

Secondary Sources

Books

Asnani, Shyam. *New Dimensions of Indian English Novel*. New Delhi: Doaba, 1987.

Beauvoir, Simone de. *The Second Sex*, trans. H.M. Parshley. New Delhi: Penguin, 1983.

Bhatnagar, Anil Kumar. *Kamala Markandaya: A Thematic Study*. New Delhi: Harman, 1996.

Bhatt, Yashoda and Yamuna Raja Rao. *The Image of Women in Indian Literature*. New Delhi: Harman, 1996.

Das, Kamala. *My Story*. New Delhi: Sterling, 1977.

Dodiya, Jaydipsinh, ed. *The Fiction of Shobha De*. New Delhi: Prestige, 2000.

Dhawan, R.K., ed. *Indian Women Novelists*. New Delhi: Prestige, 1991.

Dhawan, R.K., ed. *Indian Women Writers*. New Delhi: Prestige, 2001.

Ellis, Sarah. *The Wives of England: Their Relative Duties, Domestic Influence and Social Obligation*. New York: E. Walker, 1843.

Flora, Alexander. *Contemporary Women Novelists*. London: Edward Arnold, 1989.

Grewal, J.S. and Hugh Johnstone, ed. *The India-Canada Relationship*. New Delhi, 1994.

Gupta, G.S. Balarama. *Indian Writing in English*. Gulbarga, 1978.

Jain, N.K. *Women in Indo-Anglian Fiction: Tradition and Modernity*. New Delhi: Atlantic, 1978.

Krishna Rao, A.V. *The Indo-Anglian Novel and Changing Traditions*. Mysore: Rao and Raghavan, 1977.

Krishnaswami, Santha. *The Women in Indian Fiction*. New Delhi: Ashish, 1984.

Kulkarni, V.B. *The British Statesmen in India*. New Delhi, 1961.

Kumar, A.V. Suresh. *Six Indian Novelists: Mulk Raj Anand, Raja Rao, R.K. Narayan, B. Rajan, Kamala Markandaya, Anita Desai*. New Delhi: Pencraft International, 1999.

Mahle, H.S. *Indo-Anglian Fiction: Some Perspectives*. New Delhi: Jainsons, 1976.

Markandaya, Kamala. *A Silence of Desire*. London: Putnam, 1960.

_____. *Two Virgins*. New Delhi: Vikas, 1977.

_____. *Nectar in a Sieve*. Bombay: Jaico, 1980.

Mehta, P.P. *Indo-Anglian Fiction: An Assessment*. Bareilly: Prakash, 1968.

Mohan, Ramesh. *Indian Writing in English*. Madras, 1978.

Naik, M.K. *A History of Indian English Literature*.

Pathak, R.S., ed. *Recent Indian Fiction*,. New Delhi: Prestige, 1996.

Prasad, Madhusudan. *Indian English Novelists*. New Delhi: Sterling, 1982.

Pratt, Annis. *The Archetypal Patterns in Women's Fiction*. Bloomington: Indiana University Press, 1981.

Pritam, Amrita. *Rassedi Ticket*. New Delhi: Kitabghar, 1993.

Rajeshwar, M., ed. *The Indo-Anglian Novel and Changing Traditions*. Mysore: Rao and Raghavan, 1977.

Rao, Raja. *The Serpent and the Rope*. New Delhi: Orient, 1968.

Reddy, K Venkata. *Major Indian Novelists*. New Delhi: Prestige, 1997.

Sanyal, C. Samares. *Indianness in Major Indo-English Novels*. Bareilly: Prakash, 1984.

Saxena, O.P. *Glimpses of Indo-English*, 2 Vols. New Delhi, 1969.

Shirwadkar, Meena. *Image of Woman in Indo-Anglian Novel*. New Delhi: Sterling, 1979.

Showalter, Elaine. *The New Feminist Criticism*. New Pantheon, 1985.

Singer, Milton. *When A Great Tradition Modernises*. New Delhi: Vikas, 1972.

Singh, K.N., ed. *Indian Writing in English*. New Delhi: Heritage, 1976.

Singh, Pramod Kumar. *Indian Fiction in English*. New Delhi: Atlantic, 2000.

Singh, R.K. *Indian English Writing*. New Delhi: Harman, 1996.

Spacks, Patricia Meyer. *The Female Imagination*. New York: Avon, 1975.

Srivastava, Sharad. *The New Woman in Indian English Fiction: A Study of Kamala Markandaya, Anita Desai, Namita Gokhale and Shobha De*. New Delhi, 1996.

Stenvorth, Klaus. *The Indo-English Novel: The Impact of the West on Literature in a Developing Country*. Germany: University of Hamburg, 1983.

Suneel, Seema. *Man-Woman Relationship in Indian Fiction*. New Delhi: Prestige, 1996.

Thapar, Romila. *Ancient Indian Social History: Some Interpretations*. New Delhi, 1978.

Tong, Rosemarie. *Feminist Thought*. London: Routledge, 1993.

Verma, R.M. *Some Aspects of Indo-English Fiction*. New Delhi, 1978.

Walsh, William. *Readings in Commonwealth Literature*. Oxford University Press, 1973.

Articles

Banerjee, Lakshmisree. "Indian Women's Voices: The Post Colonial and Post Modernist Era," *The Commonwealth Review*, Vol. VII, No. 2, 1995-96

Bhargav, Simran and Madhu Jain. "Married Women: Changing Sexuality," *India Today*, 15 Oct. 1989.

Chaddah, R.P. "The Partition in Indo-Anglian Fiction," *Journal of Indian Writing in English*, Vol. 5, No. 2, July 1977.

Desai, Anita. "Secret Connivance," *Times Literary Supplement*, 14 September, 1990.

Gupta, G.S. Balarama. "Studies in Indian Fiction in English," *Journal of Indian Writing in English*, 1985.

Hoskote, Ranjit. "Dawning of the New De," *Times of India*, 2 Feb. 1995.

Jain, Madhu. "Cat on a Cold Tin Roof," *India Today*, Oct. 15, 1989.

John B. Alphonso-Karkala. "Indo-English Fiction," *Literature East and West*, 8, No. 1 (Winter 1964).

Khuswal, M.S. "A Neglected Area of Indo-Anglian Writing in English," *Journal of Indian Writers*, Vol. 6, No. 1, Jan. 1978.

Lal. P. "Nostalgia Indo-Anglia," *Journal of Indian Writing in English*, No. 3, Jan. 1975.

Lukacs, Georg. "Approximation to Life in the Novel and the Play," *Sociology of Literature and Drama*, ed. Elizabeth and Tom Burns. Penguin, 1973.

Mukherjee, Meenakshi. "English in India," *Literacy Landscape in India and Foreign Review* (Aug. 1, 1972).

Narasimhaiah, C.D. "Women in Fiction by Women—An Introductory Talk," *The Literary Criterion*, 20.4 (1985).

Ramamurthy, K.S. "The Puranic Tradition and Modern Indo-Anglian Fiction," *Indian Writing Today*, II, IV (Jan.-March, 1970).

Ramachandran, Janaki. "Survival Tactics," *The Hindu*, Feb. 2, 1977.

Sethi, Sunil. "De in, De out," *Seminar*, 387, August 1991.

Shah, A.B. "Indian Tradition and Modernity," *Quest*, XL, VI (Monsoon 1965), 9-19.

Shahane, Vasant A. "Indo-Anglian Fiction and the Question of Form," *Journal of Indian Writing in English*, 2, No. 2, July 1979.

Sirour, Ariya. "The Crisis in Indo-Anglian Fiction: The Linguistic Aspect," *Commonwealth Quaterly*, Dec. 1978.

Surendran, C.P. "Just Another De," *The Illustrated Weekly of India*, 6 Nov. 1992.

Trehan, Madhu and Sunil Sethi. "A Time for Reckoning," *India Today*, 15 August 1980.

Verghese, Paul C. "Problem of the Indian Novelists in English," *The Banasthali Patrika*, No. 12, Jan. 1969.

White, Robin. "Fiction in India," *The Reporter*, 28, No. 4, 1963.

Index